The British Virgin Islands

An Introduction and Guide

Claudia Colli

MACMILLAN
CARIBBEAN

Macmillan Education

Between Towns Road, Oxford OX4 3PP
A division of Macmillan Publishers Limited
Companies and representatives throughout the world

www.macmillan-caribbean.com

ISBN 978–1–4050–2862–2

Typeset by CjB Editorial Plus
Cover design by Gary Fielder, AC Design
Cover photographs by Jim Scheiner

The author and publishers would like to thank the following for permission to
reproduce their photographs: Jim Scheiner, all photos except for:
John Binns / National Parks Trust, page 119; Claudia Colli, pages 25, 62, 75, 115;
Dive BVI, Virgin Gorda, page 89; Penny Haycraft, pages 36, 38 (bottom);
Alan Smith, pages 55, 82, 122.

The author and publishers wish to thank the following rights holders for the use of
copyright material:
Jim Rogers for the extract from *The Geological origins of the British Virgin Islands*
by Jim Rogers; Charles Helsley for the adapted text from an unpublished thesis
titled 'Geology of the British Virgin Islands' by Charles E Helsley, PhD. dissertation,
Princeton University, Princeton, New Jersey, 1960

If any copyright holders have been omitted, please contact the publishers who will
make the necessary arrangements at the first opportunity.

Printed and bound in Malaysia
2011 2010 2009 2008 2007
10 9 8 7 6 5 4 3 2

▲ Sitting beneath a palm on Salt Island

Contents

Foreword

The complaint is often voiced by those doing research for literary, academic or journalistic work on the BVI that there is very little written material on the territory 'out there'. For that reason alone, this guidebook by Claudia Colli will be warmly welcomed as an addition to a scarce literary resource base. But it is much more than just that.

Written by an American who adopted, and was adopted by, the BVI and can thus lay claim to the description 'British Virgin Islander' in its widest sense, *The British Virgin Islands* will be a useful reference tool not only for the prospective visitor but also for islanders and residents, both recent and long term. I can see it also being useful in schools for the social studies teacher, and a welcome addition to school and home libraries.

The writer is unabashedly in love with her adopted home, and it comes through on nearly every page. The historical, geographical and geological introductory chapters pack a lot of pertinent information into a small space. Visitors will find the chapters on bushes, trees, fruits and vegetables of real value and interest. Again, many people who live in the BVI have probably not seen this information written down in one place before, and will enjoy the experience. As with any self-respecting guidebook, however, the chapters on touring, things to do, places to visit (including national parks and ruins), are particularly strong. It is testimony to Ms Colli's hard work, painstaking research and literary sense that she is able to bring so much, historical and contemporary, together in this way.

Claudia Colli has succeeded in an ambitious project of combining diverse pieces of information in one easily readable mosaic of a guidebook. In doing so, and in her choice of content, she has performed a valuable service to the British Virgin Islands and to its visitors and residents.

Elton Georges, CMG
Deputy Governor, British Virgin Islands, 1984–2004

Acknowledgement

Writing this book has been an intense and rewarding experience. I have lived in the British Virgin Islands for many years, and as an author and editor based in the BVI have spent countless hours writing about these beautiful islands and their special nature. This book, though, has given me the opportunity to write about them much more comprehensively: to produce an in-depth look at their history, culture, sites and beauty. These islands are indeed special and I hope to convey this notion to a wide audience.

There are many people to thank. First of all, Sonia Williams and Aragorn Dick-Read for suggesting that I take on the project. My husband Alan has been a patient supporter and an objective critic through many months of preparation and writing. I don't know how I could have completed this book without his wonderful cooking.

I would especially like to thank Elton Georges for his wisdom and guidance and Gail Bruce for her editing skills. Photographer and BVI resident Jim Scheiner supplied the majority of the photograhs, and his contribution has given the book much of its visual impact. I would like to express my appreciation to Clive Petrovich, Jim Rogers, Mitch Kent, Nancy Woodfield and the late Michael Arneborg for their expertise and invaluable comments; as well as to Julia Donovan for her assistance with the preparation of photos and maps.

I would like to dedicate this book to my husband Alan, my sons, Brandon and Jason, and the people of the British Virgin Islands.

Claudia Colli 2006

❶ Getting to know us

An introduction to the British Virgin Islands

Rising dramatically out of crystal blue waters, the British Virgin Islands are among the most visually stunning islands in the Caribbean. Their unique geography has grouped this series of 40 or so islands, islets and cays in close proximity, creating a serpentine chain of emerald and turquoise.

What sets the British Virgin Islands apart from many of its Caribbean neighbours are its sheltered sailing waters. The BVI's many closely positioned islands ensure that the seas are never too rough for a comfortable sail and that the next port of call is a mere hour or two's sail away.

The British Virgin Islands' main waterway is the Sir Francis Drake Channel, named after the famous explorer who used the route to launch his attack on the Spanish armada anchored in nearby Puerto

▲ An aerial view of Virgin Gorda's North Sound and surrounding islands

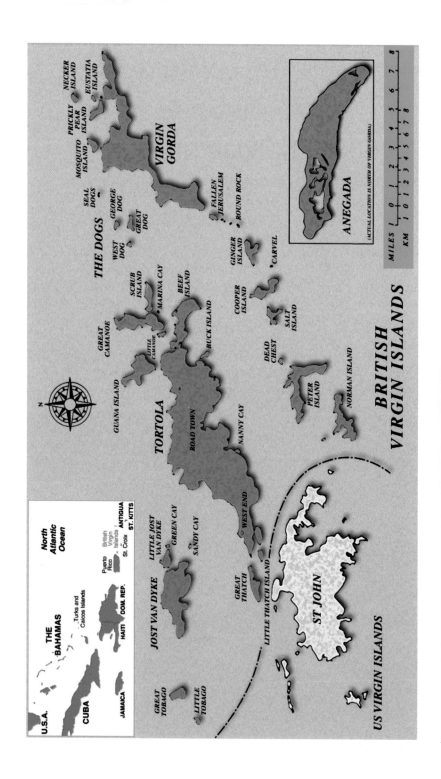

BRITISH
VIRGIN ISLANDS

Rico. Today the same channel is sailed by dozens of modern-day explorers, charter yachtsmen in quest of a tropical cocktail in one of the area's many picturesque anchorages. The territory virtually pioneered the concept of bareboating (a charter yacht without captain or crew) and since the first company based itself here in the late 1960s, the BVI has become home to the region's largest bareboat flotilla.

A British territory, with a locally elected government, the BVI is among the most stable countries in the region and boasts one of its highest per capita incomes. The introduction of legislation governing international companies in the early 1980s, expert promotion and sound regulation have made it an international finance centre, and balancing these twin pillars – tourism and finance – has been the formula of the territory's economic success.

But for all its sophistication, the BVI retains its small-island charm. Its hillsides rise vertically from the sea, its beaches with their long swaths of powdery sand are among the Caribbean's most beautiful, and its waters are so vibrant and clear you'll wonder how you can swim anywhere else again.

The British Virgin Islands has always prided itself on being different. In today's bustling and over-stressed world, the territory offers an enviable lifestyle, one that is slower paced and a little more gracious. The BVI is a place where people take the time to say 'Good morning' when you pass them in the street and where you may have to slow your car down for a herd of goats crossing the road.

The BVI is often referred to as one of 'Nature's little secrets'. In today's world of the Internet and glossy travel magazines, it's hard to keep a secret. But there

▲ The BVI lifestyle is slower paced and more gracious

are still plenty of things left to discover. The islands offer dozens of attractions and places of natural beauty to visit, as well as scores of activities such as sailing, diving and hiking to keep you occupied. As you read on, you will learn more about the BVI's history, its culture, geography, flora and fauna – just a few of the attributes that make these islands a place of both sophistication and simplicity.

ABOUT THE ISLANDS

The British Virgin Islands are like a large and robust family. Whether quiet or flamboyant, mountainous or flat, each island contributes its own unique nature to the mix. Tortola, the largest of the islands, is the dominant sibling of the group. It is the seat of government and centre of commerce, and has the largest population. Virgin Gorda, a gracious isle of high-end resorts, guest villas and fabulous beaches, has the next largest population, followed by lightly populated and picture-pretty Jost Van Dyke. Anegada is the one that dares to be different. While the others are mountainous and green, Anegada is a flat, sandy isle that stands apart from its statuesque relations. Then there are the cousins, dozens of them. Some are mere rocks or sandy spits, while others are small green islands containing a hotel or a few guest houses, each with its own charm and character.

▲ A view from Peter Island's Deadman's Bay to Tortola

In all, the 40 or so islands of the group cover 59 square miles (155 square km), making up a small island nation that is ideally positioned, easy to reach, yet just far enough away to seem remote. Located 60 miles (97 km) east of Puerto Rico and 1,100 miles (1,769 km) southeast of Miami, the BVI is bordered by the Atlantic Ocean to the north and the Caribbean Sea to the south. It is part of the same geographical group as its closest neighbour, the US Virgin Islands, and the main islands in these two territories, Tortola in the BVI and St Thomas in the USVI, are just 10 miles (16 km) apart. Competing political interests though, have through the centuries divided these isles into the separate national groupings we now know as the US and British Virgin Islands. Even so, culture, family ties and commerce still unite these two sets of Virgins, and ferries depart from both the US and British Virgin Islands filled with islanders travelling on business or to visit family and friends.

▲ Cane Garden Bay at sunset

GETTING HERE

Although there are no direct flights to the BVI from the US mainland or Europe, getting to the British Virgin Islands is easy. San Juan, Puerto Rico acts as a hub for flights arriving from the United States and elsewhere in the Caribbean, and a 30-minute trip aboard one of several dozen daily inter-island flights links Puerto Rico to the Terrence B. Lettsome International Airport on Beef Island. A bridge connects Beef Island to Tortola.

Travellers from the US can also fly into neighbouring St Thomas in the US Virgin Islands and take a scenic 45-minute ferry ride, a relaxing alternative to flying. UK visitors can fly into Antigua and those from France, into St Martin. Both islands have scheduled flights to the BVI.

Getting around the BVI's many islands by air is also easy. Intra-island flights connect Beef Island to Virgin Gorda and Anegada, and there are ferries between Tortola and Virgin Gorda and Jost Van Dyke as well as some of the resort islands.

HOW THE ISLANDS WERE FORMED

When you first arrive in the BVI, you'll notice its verticality. There seems to be only two directions to the British Virgin Islands, up or down, and for a tourist arriving from the airport, the taxi trip can be an exhilarating one as the driver negotiates a series of steep hills and hairpin turns. This steepness is no casual act of nature, but the result of massive subterranean pressures over the course of millions of years.

Our dramatic archipelago of palm studded islands, which lies at the northern end of the island chain that stretches from South America northwards, was not created by recent volcanic eruption as in other nearby regions of the Caribbean, but rather by a slower and more methodical process. As you drive around Tortola, you will see evidence of its sedimentary nature in the cliff faces that were exposed when many of its roads were excavated, and which now offer a fascinating glimpse of the BVI's prehistoric formation.

Our geology is complex, influenced by dynamic forces located deep within the earth. In the simplest of terms, the Virgin Islands are situated on a foundation of sea-floor basalt flows that were deposited more than 80 million years ago. Later, many thousands of feet of volcanic sediments accumulated on these flows. Most of these volcanic sediments were deposited in almost horizontal layers, but through powerful uplifts were tilted to a near-vertical position (as seen in those cliff faces).

▲ The dramatic granite boulders of The Baths

The forces that created the spectacular boulders of the Virgin Gorda Baths, and some of the other large granite outcrops that are scattered around the BVI, are especially intriguing. About 40 million years ago, the insertion of hot liquid magma (now called the Virgin Gorda Batholith) created uplift of the ancient sea floor. As the sea floor was exposed and weathered over the millennia, massive crystalline granite rocks were exposed, gradually decaying in the incessant surf. Over the intervening years, the slabs split into smaller sections. Poised atop one another in seemingly precarious positions and weathered by the sea and the wind, these boulders formed The Baths as we know them today. This amazing acrobatic feat has produced a labyrinth of grottoes and sheltered sea pools, which are now a world famous attraction.

At one time when sea levels were lower, our islands were probably joined, but as the sea rose, all that remained were the tops of the mountains upon which we now live. The exception to this is Anegada, the BVI's only coral atoll. Anegada, which is located to the northeast of the island chain, is limestone in origin. Like most atolls, Anegada began as a circular coral reef, which over the millennia gradually filled in with sediment. Ringed with sandy beaches, Anegada is a mere 28 feet (8.5 metres) above sea level at its highest point.

The formation of the Virgin Islands is still far from complete. The Puerto Rico trench, a major mobile submarine fault situated just to

▲ Yachts anchor off the Indians

the west of the Virgin Islands, ensures that the region's geology is not static. Over the next millennia, beaches will come and go, mountains will erode and new ones form. Like a massive piece of sculpture, the Virgin Islands are a work in progress.

The British Virgin Islands have benefited from their unique geography enormously. It has helped influence much of the territory's history and continues to direct its current course. Traditionally British Virgin Islanders have relied on the sea. It has acted as their highway, means of communication and source of food. Today, these sheltered waters are the highway that transports visitors to the islands and are what have helped make the BVI a major yachting and tourism centre.

For a more in-depth look at the geology of the Virgin Islands, see the Appendix on page 150: 'The Geological Origins of the Virgin Islands' by Jim Rogers.

② A pastiche of cultures

The BVI's people and heritage

British Virgin Islanders are a diverse group of people. With so many islands, how could they not be? In addition to native-born British Virgin Islanders, each of these islands is also composed of a melange of people from isles throughout the West Indies. Ask an islander where he or she is from and the answer may be, 'My mother was born here, but my father is from Grenada' – or Antigua, Dominica or St Vincent. With development comes immigration, and over the years, trading and aspirations for a better life have kept islanders on the move.

Traditionally, British Virgin Islanders were farmers and fishermen, a resourceful and industrious folk who made a living out of the rocky soil and from the surrounding sea. Their ancestors were brought here from Africa as slaves to work the cotton and sugar plantations that were the mainstay of the islands' colonial economy. Slaves were

▲ A fisherman lays a trap

emancipated in the British West Indies in 1834 and the British planters in the BVI abandoned the islands soon afterwards, but their former workers remained behind. The plantation land which was gradually subdivided was acquired by these hardworking people and turned into small agricultural plots, making British Virgin Islanders some of the largest native landholders in the Caribbean.

Land ownership has given BV Islanders a sense of pride and resilience that has carried them through some tough times. The post-plantation economy was never strong and support from Britain meagre, making life here, to a large extent, one of subsistence.

Much of the Virgin Islanders' character has been bred by the self-sufficiency created by isolation. For centuries, the islands were linked to each other and the outside world only by the sea. People travelled between islands by locally built island sloops or later by small diesel-powered cargo boats that transported fruits and vegetables to nearby islands. Because of the mountainous terrain, even communities on the same islands were cut off from one another, and were only accessible by donkey or horse along narrow mountain tracks, or again, by boat.

▲ British Virgin Islands hat maker, Estelle Dawson

Strong family ties and religious belief have both been important to British Virgin Islanders over the last two centuries, and it is no different today. Extended families are large and friendships are important. On a small island everyone knows everyone else, and as a matter of course, weddings and funerals are big events with hundreds of people attending. Elderly parents live with their adult children, and grandparents taking care of the grandchildren – a tradition that has died out in many parts of the developed world – is still prevalent here.

Life changed significantly for British Virgin Islanders in the last half of the twentieth century. The largely rural economy slowly gave way to a new industry, tourism, and this once isolated nation was thrust onto the global stage. New cultures took root as immigrants from other islands arrived to augment local workers in the hotels, charter boat companies and the burgeoning construction industry. Tourists, along with settlers from mainly the UK and North America, added to this mix with their own set of values, preoccupations and needs.

Education was now a priority on these islands where children had largely been taught in small schools run by the churches. A government-supported primary and secondary school system, which started in the 1940s, was greatly expanded in the late 1960s. In 1990 the H. Lavity Stoutt Community College was established to help islanders compete for the managerial and technical jobs that were now created. This became especially important with the rapid development of the territory's offshore finance industry.

Once primarily farmers and fishermen, today British Virgin Islanders work as hotel managers and receptionists; yacht skippers and maintenance workers. They run trust companies and consulting firms. And yes, a few still farm and fish. British Virgin Islanders have moved forward, but their heritage lives on.

FESTIVAL

British Virgin Islands culture is a pastiche of African, West Indian and British influences. It has developed since slave times with an oral tradition of folk stories and history passed down from parent to child. The BVI's biggest cultural celebration is its August Emancipation Festival, which in fact begins in the middle of July. Festival's roots began with the Emancipation Proclamation, which according to tradition, was read out on the first Monday of August, 1834 at Road Town's Sunday Morning Well. The Proclamation was followed by an island-wide celebration, the likes of which the islands had never seen. There were church picnics, horse races and watersports. Children unfurled maypoles and adults danced in the streets.

For decades this tradition was carried on annually in August, but it wasn't until the 1950s that it became the festival-like event that we know today. The year that Queen Elizabeth ascended the throne in England, 1952, was marked here in the British Virgin Islands by a carnival parade that slowly made its way down the Main Street of Road Town. People danced and wore bright and colourful clothing

▲ A colourful troupe dances its way down the street at the Festival parade

and costumes. So popular was the event that the next year it was decided to incorporate a parade into the August festivities and eventually Festival was declared a three-day public holiday. The first Monday in August would be parade day; the next day was set aside for horse racing and watersports and on Wednesday, East End and Long Look on Tortola would stage their own affair with parades and activities. The event continued to grow and a Festival Village, a collection of colourful booths serving local food and drink, was constructed each year in the midst of Road Town. The Village soon became an entertainment centre for the festivities, featuring popular local and regional reggae and soca bands.

Today Festival is organized by a government committee and dozens of community organizations and individuals. Festival's roots as an emancipation celebration have been newly emphasized and one of the highlights of the event is a re-enactment of the Emancipation Proclamation at the Sunday Morning Well, now a popular community gathering spot. Dressed in traditional African garb, members of the churches and prominent community representatives give speeches, recite prayers of thanksgiving, and of course, read out the famous

▼ A young parade participant flashes a smile

Proclamation. Recently, the quiet village of Carrot Bay also jumped on the Festival bandwagon, tagging on its own fiesta at the end of the week.

Cultural roots aside, Festival in the BVI is one tremendous party – a two week-long celebration of life and a year of hard work. People dance in the street, dress in their brightest clothes, drink rum and maubi, and play music amplified to the hilt. At J'ouvert – also called the Rise and Shine Tramp – the street dancing begins before dawn and carries on through the early morning. The highlight of Festival is August Monday, the day of the Grand Parade. Dozens of costumed troupes, many representing community organizations; massive trucks carrying a battalion of musicians and amplification equipment; colourful Mocko Jumbies dancing atop tall stilts; beauty queens, princes and princesses, all wend their way down Road Town's waterfront road. Fun to participate in and fun to watch, Festival is as much a national state of mind as an event.

THE SOUNDS OF THE BVI

Music and the West Indies are almost synonymous. Played loud and exuberantly, music is a cultural necessity, a bit like breathing fresh air. While some of the musical forms are pure British Virgin Islands,

▲ Local entertainer, Quito Rymer

others are hybrids, brought here from other islands and made into a distinctive BVI sound.

Unlike reggae and other types of island music, **Fungi** is a Virgin Islands original. This indigenous form of scratch band music has been a centrepiece of local culture for over a century. Traditionally, fungi band instruments were fashioned from easily gathered materials and commonplace instruments: shakers made from gourds; a bass from a wash pan; strings and a stick; simple flutes, guitars and banjos. Today keyboards and amplification are occasionally added.

Steelband music originated in Trinidad, but this imported musical form is now a large part of the BVI's musical tradition. The steel pans are created from discarded oil barrels, the tops of which are hammered into a concave shape to create varying tones and keys. This popular type of music is kept alive throughout the islands by the BVI High School and a variety of community groups who organize bands and lessons for young people.

A steel drum band entertains guests on Peter Island

15

Calypso, another Trinidadian import, is also popular here, especially during Festival when there are regular local and international competitions. Calypso originated as a form of social protest. Through music, slaves could criticize or make fun of their masters discreetly. Over the years, calypso has taken on a political edge and has become a form of social and political criticism and comment.

Reggae may have originated in Jamaica, the land of musical legends, Bob Marley and Jimmy Cliff, but here in the BVI, it has its own identity. BVI reggae mixes popular music, local themes and a traditional reggae beat. **Soca** is a subtle variation of reggae and calypso, although louder and brasher. Both reggae and soca are great to dance to and most evenings in the BVI you can find a popular band playing at a local club or restaurant.

DANCE TO THE MUSIC

The Heritage Dancers have kept alive forms of dance that were popular here in the nineteenth and early part of the twentieth centuries. Some of the dances reflect ones brought back from the Dominican Republic by BV Islanders who from time to time emigrated there to work the cane fields, sending home money when times in the BVI were particularly hard. One of these popular dances is the Meringue, which is believed by some to have started as a peasant dance in the Dominican Republic by African slaves. Another is the Quadrille, which owes its roots to the French, although by the mid-1850s it became popular in England, America and the West Indies. The dancers wear costumes that are a creative combination of traditional nineteenth-century BVI dress and the colourful dress of the Dominican Republic. The women wear turbans and dresses with full, ruffled skirts and shirred bodices; the men, white or black pants and loose shirts.

Elsewhere, dancing in the Virgin Islands is free-style and unabashed. Virgin Islanders dance to reggae, fungi and soca, shaking their hips and sashaying throughout the dance floor. BV Islanders dance their way down the road during the Festival parade and up and down the streets through the early morning hours at J'ouvert.

LOCAL TASTES: FOODS OF THE BVI

When you think of food in the BVI, think different. Although many restaurants here serve international fare, you won't have fully experienced BVI culture until you have sampled some of its food. Local

A good day's catch ▶

food has evolved from a combination of that which has been introduced here from Britain and from other Caribbean islands, and what will grow in our finicky tropical climate. West Indian food is filling, a bit heavy on the carbohydrates, yet nourishing. It's also fun to experience some cuisine anomalies like fruits used as vegetables, and wonder whether the yam on your plate is really a yam or a sweet potato. No matter what you eat, though, you will not leave a local restaurant hungry.

Some of the most common foods that you might encounter here are called ground provisions – hardy root crops such as sweet potato, tannia (similar to a sweet potato), cassava and yams. Provisions, along with squashes, pumpkin and tropical fruits that in their unripe stage are boiled and used as vegetables, are among the staple items of the BVI diet. Green papaya is also used as vegetable here, boiled, cut up into pieces and served with butter and sautéed onions. Fried plantain is another common side dish. This large and starchy banana is peeled and sautéed in butter. Fungi, a dish of cornmeal similar to the Italian dish of polenta, is a food handed down from slave times.

In a land surrounded by sea, fish is abundant. Some of the most popular fish here are those known as potfish – fish such as yellow tail and 'goutou' (the local name for parrot fish), which are generally caught in locally made fish traps. Other commonly served fish are trigger fish, also known as 'old wife' and king fish, a pelagic fish that is a popular catch in sport fishing competitions. Other deep water fish that you might find on your plate are tuna, wahoo, swordfish and dolphin (often referred to as mahi mahi to differentiate it from the marine mammal of the same name). Fishermen often signal their return with a successful catch by blowing a conch shell, and a large crowd will usually gather by the side of the boat to buy the fish before it is unloaded. On occasion you may also see fishermen selling their catch from the back of a truck by the Road Town roundabout. Either way, you have to be fast, since the fish go quickly.

Lobster, a clawless variety, is popular in the BVI and several restaurants keep them fresh in tanks. One of the most delicious and unusual sea foods here is conch. This shellfish, which is found in those beautiful large conch shells popular in gift shops, is stewed with tomatoes, onions, garlic and fresh thyme or served in rotis or patties.

In addition to fruits and vegetables, BVI farmers raise a variety of livestock which eventually turn up in local stews. Goat, mutton and beef are all popular, as is stewed or fried chicken. Although chickens are raised in the BVI, as you can see from the number running freely along the roads, most are imported.

The food of the BVI is derived from numerous Caribbean and European influences. The popular johnny cake comes from the traditional English food known as a journey cake. Travellers along the English post roads would take this easily transported disc of fried dough along with them as part of their provisions. Salt fish made from salted cod is also a standard European food used on long sea journeys before refrigeration. Pattie, or paté as it is sometimes called, is a bit like a Cornish pasty. Here, the pastries often contain spicy fillings of minced beef, saltfish or chicken and are generally fried. Curried foods, such as goat or chicken, are also prevalent. Curry was introduced by Guyanese and Trinidadian immigrants of East Indian origin. The most common Trinidadian dish found in the BVI is roti. Originally this Indian bread was filled with leftover curry and taken into the cane fields of Trinidad by the workers as an easily transportable lunch.

SPORTS

BV Islanders are passionate about sports. **Football** in the BVI (as it is in most parts of the world except the United States) means soccer, and it is played here with zeal. There is a national team and there is a national junior team, both of which play locally and regionally. The A. O. Shirley recreation ground in Road Town is the site of soccer matches and other athletic and sporting events such as track, rugby, basketball and softball. A gymnasium and multipurpose centre can also be found here.

On Sunday afternoons you may see the genteel sport of cricket being played in the field across the road. If it's an important game, the players, often from some of the 'down islands' such as St Kitts and Nevis, will be dressed in classic white kit. **Rugby** is also played here, but generally by the British population; a game against the British Navy when it is in port can be a rough and tumble affair. American sports like basketball and softball are also popular. The BVI may be small, but it nonetheless has some world class athletes and the territory is routinely represented in track and field events at the Olympics, the Pan American Games and the Caribbean Games.

Among the most popular sports in the territory is **horse racing**. People are serious about their horses and import thoroughbreds from elsewhere in the Caribbean and the US. Horse races are held at the race track at Sea Cows Bay several times a year, including the first Tuesday in August during Festival. **Dominoes** is not a sport, but in the BVI it's approached with similar enthusiasm. The sound of dominoes being slapped down on a home-made table is a familiar sound outside homes and roadside bars.

▲ The horse races at the race track at Sea Cows Bay

BRITISH HERITAGE

How British are the British Virgin Islands? To look around the supermarkets stocked with American goods, or listen to the radio broadcasting reggae, soca and salsa you might say, 'not very'. In some ways you would be right. The BVI's currency is the US dollar, a convenience brought about by the territory's close links to the US Virgin Islands; its television programmes originate from the US mainland; and its culture and many of its foods are rooted in the West Indies. But in many other ways, the BVI remains firmly British.

▲ A Royal Virgin Islands policeman

▲ The maker of the log boat boasts that it is 'British made'

The BVI became a colony of England in 1672, and has been administered by British commissioners, administrators and governors from that time until the present. In recent decades though, a locally elected government has taken on a much greater role in the territory's administration.

What is left from the BVI's early colonial days is just enough pomp and ceremony to make the islands feel British, although not in an overt way. Several of the islands' holidays are rooted in English tradition, as is its spelling, its enthusiasm for sports like cricket and rugby and a fondness for some of its cuisine including johnny, or journey cakes, and meat patties.

The Queen is still a notable figure here and her birthday is marked with a parade in Road Town overseen by the Governor, members of the local government and prominent members of the community. Troops of Boy Scouts, Girl Guides, members of the Red Cross and community groups march in the small parade held at the New Recreation Ground in Road Town.

Later in the day, a cocktail party is held at the Governor's official residence in Road Town. Members of the Royal Virgin Islands Police give a formal salute and the Union Jack is lowered as guests sing *God Save the Queen*. New members of the Order of the British Empire are usually announced on this day, an honour that is bestowed on British Virgin Islands residents who have given outstanding service to the territory.

The Queen has visited the territory twice – each visit celebrated with a tropically flavoured fanfare. Her first visit in 1966 coincided with a spurt of development that included the paving of the BVI airport on Beef Island and the construction of a new road to Tortola's West End along the island's jagged southwestern coastline, a route that formerly went over the mountains. She also officially opened the Queen Elizabeth Bridge, a single-lane draw bridge linking Beef Island to Tortola.

In 1977, the Queen, along with Prince Phillip, arrived for a second visit aboard the royal yacht *Britannia*. The occasion was marked with a parade down the waterfront road, with the Queen travelling in a white Lincoln Continental provided by a resident hotel owner. Other royal visitors to the islands have included the Queen Mother, Princess Anne, Prince Charles and Prince Andrew, each visit adding a note of excitement to the islands, as well as a welcome flurry of road paving and beautification projects.

❸ Through the years
A historical perspective

For a British Virgin Islands history buff, discovering a piece of Amerindian pottery, the stone wall of a plantation house, or the boiling vat from a rum distillery is as rewarding as finding a chest filled with gold doubloons. A fragment of the past unearthed is indeed a treasure, one that can yield a greater understanding of the present.

The BVI's history may be briefer than that of the ancient cultures of Africa, Asia or the Middle East, but nonetheless, a lot has happened in its 2,000 years or so of habitation. The history of the British Virgin Islands is peppered with drama, and spiced with the deeds and actions of a colourful cast of characters: Indian chiefs, bold explorers, marauding pirates and pioneering planters. It is also a saga of the early sugar and rum trade, competing national interests and a people who emerged from slavery to take the future into their own hands. Young and formative, the BVI has only begun to tell its story.

THE AMERINDIANS

The first characters to enter the BVI's historical stage were the Amerindians. Originally from the Orinoco Basin in what is today Venezuela, the Indians travelled up through the Lesser Antilles by dugout canoe before the time of Christ and settled in what is now the British Virgin Islands, probably around 600 BC. The first settlers were nomadic people, who fished in small canoes and collected shellfish from the shoreline.

Gathering fruit and vegetables from the thick forests that once covered the entire Virgin Islands, these pre-ceramic people had no permanent villages. Around 900 AD, these early tribes were replaced by a more sophisticated group who established villages in coastal areas throughout the British Virgin Islands. Thirty-two sites have been surveyed on Tortola alone and over 1,000 Amerindians may have lived here at this time.

The Indian tribes who settled in the region, referred to as the Eastern Taino, were primarily a fisher-folk who, like the nomadic tribes before them, used dugouts to catch fish offshore and gathered shellfish from nearby mangrove swamps and lagoons. These first inhabitants lived in large communal round houses supported by massive wooden posts covered in grasses and palm leaves. They ground cassava into flour and made it into a flat bread baked on round pottery griddles placed upon hearths fuelled with charcoal. They fashioned jewellery out of shells and wove cotton for their clothing.

Religion was fundamental to the Amerindians, who worshipped *zemis* – deities that they believed inhabited objects in nature, such as trees and rocks. The two supreme deities were Yúcahu, the lord of cassava and the sea and Atabey, his mother, who was the goddess of fresh water and fertility. *Zemis* were also represented by three-cornered objects formed from stone, shell or pottery. Tribes were headed by caciques or chiefs, who also presided over their religious life, which revolved around elaborate and festive ceremonies incorporating dancing, music and hallucinogenic drugs.

Sports and religion were combined in a unique ball game that was played upon a rectangular ball court marked by carved stones. The ball was made of hard rubber and was kept in constant motion,

Archaeology in action

The mystery of the BVI's earliest people is being unravelled by a team of archaeologists from the London University's Institute of Archaeology. Dr Peter Drewett was first invited to the BVI in 1995 to excavate a site at the H. Lavity Stoutt Community College at Paraquita Bay on Tortola, where he found the remains of a temporary fishing camp.

The team was soon attracted to a site on Belmont on the island's northwestern shore, where an earlier survey had unearthed many significant artefacts including large clay bowls and tools. The site

▲ Dr Peter Drewett and assistant unearth a ball court stone at the Amerindian site at Belmont

was a perfect location for an Amerindian settlement. It lies just at the back of Long Bay, giving the Indians access to the sea for fishing, and is adjacent to a Salt Pond, which in Amerindian times was probably a freshwater inlet linked to the sea, an ideal source for shellfish such as whelk and crabs.

Since 1996, Dr Drewett's month-long visits have revealed that the area was once a vibrant Amerindian village and religious ceremonial centre. Working along with Dr Drewett is his wife Lysbeth, also an archaeologist from London University, Dr Brian Bates from Longwood University in Virginia, USA, and a phalanx of archaeological students from London and Longwood Universities.

Among the treasure trove of artefacts discovered on the site have been decorated clay bowls, some with *adornos* (a decorated figure on the bowl rim); spinning whorls, used in the making of cotton fibre for weaving; and stone and shell tools. Over their years of excavation, the archaeologists have uncovered an impressive 8,000 pieces of pottery – most broken, although quite a few whole or near whole. Their most significant discovery, though, is that the area was used as a ritual centre.

The focus of this ceremonial site is Belmont, a triangular-shaped hill that was worshipped as a *zemi*. Locally known as Sugar Loaf, the hill probably featured in a ceremony that celebrated the solstice. Polished oblong stones excavated in the ritual area line up with the centre of the hill, and on the summer solstice, the sun sets directly behind the hill, its rays cascading down the edges of the hill in an ethereal shower of light. Although the event may have been spiritual in nature, it may also have been a way of denoting the time of year, a calendar of sorts. In addition to the stones, many other artefacts have been unearthed in the area, including ritual pots and a vomit spatula (used in ceremonies to cleanse the spirit). Large numbers of fish bones and shellfish remains have also been discovered on the site, indicating that great feasts were held during these rituals.

The recent discovery of a ball court has added yet another piece to our picture of the Indian way of life. The ball court was about 82 feet (25 metres) long and 26 feet (8 metres) wide (smaller than ones found in other areas of the Caribbean), and the boundaries were marked by a series of stones, some of which are carved. More than just an athletic event to the Amerindians, these ball games were yet another part of the religious rites of the BVI's earliest inhabitants.

bounced from player to player or onto the ground with any part of the body except hands or feet. There could be ten to 30 players on a team and both men and women played the game (although not at the same time).

No one is sure what happened to the Amerindians in the British Virgin Islands. Columbus came in contact with an Indian settlement when he landed at Salt River on St Croix on his second voyage to the New World in 1493. But as he sailed northward into the islands that would later comprise the British Virgins, he mentions no Indian sightings, although they may have just remained hidden within the islands' dense forest canopy.

By the time the first settlers arrived in the British Virgin Islands, no outward traces of Amerindian settlements remained. One possible explanation for their disappearance is that they succumbed to the same European diseases that decimated hundreds of thousands of Indians in the Spanish islands. Although today little physical evidence of the Amerindians' existence in the Virgin Islands remains, remnants of their culture can be found in such local foods as cassava, in the wild cotton plants that were once used to weave their clothing, and in the English language. Words such as canoe, cannibal, hurricane, hammock and barbecue are all derived from Amerindian languages.

COLUMBUS SAILS BY

When Columbus came across the Virgin Islands in 1493, he found a sprinkling of sheltered islands. According to popular belief, he named them 'Las Once Mil Las Virgines' after the legendary St Ursula, who along with 11,000 virgins was martyred at the hands of the Huns in the fourth century. Perhaps Columbus's fanciful name was inspired by the islands' untouched beauty, or just as likely, it was a way of amplifying his discovery for the benefit of King Ferdinand and Queen Isabella of Spain, his expedition's sponsors.

Columbus's interest in the Virgin Islands was only fleeting; the Spanish had their eyes set on richer booty, and they bypassed the chain for Hispaniola and Puerto Rico, where they hoped to find gold. It is believed by some though, that the Spanish briefly occupied the Coppermine area of Virgin Gorda, where they established a mine to prospect for gold and copper. For the next 150 years, the British Virgin Islands were largely ignored by the colonial nations. The soil was considered rocky and infertile, there were no valuable minerals and the mountainous terrain was largely unsuitable for raising cattle and other livestock. As a matter of fact, one observer of the time disparagingly noted that the islands were 'wholly uninhabited, sandy, barren and craggy'.

From the sixteenth until the eighteenth centuries, piracy was rampant in the Caribbean. Spurred by the sight of gold-laden galleons sailing between the Americas and Europe, buccaneers scoured the seas looking for vulnerable ships to plunder. Taking advantage of the Virgin Islands' many sheltered coves and uncharted reefs, some of the Caribbean's most dubious characters launched their raids from BVI shores, and several islands were named after the adventurers that frequented local waters. Little Thatch took its name from Edward Teach, more commonly known as Blackbeard, whose long braided beard and lascivious reputation for having 14 wives have made him one of pirate lore's most colourful figures. Norman Island received its name from the buccaneer Norman, a dashing figure who is believed by many to have buried the booty from a plundered Spanish frigate on this desolate island just southwest of Road Harbour. The legend of buried treasure on Norman has persisted over the years, fuelled by the belief that Robert Louis Stevenson used the isle as the setting for his famous novel of piracy and intrigue, *Treasure Island*. A series of caves on the island's northwestern point have encouraged this story, and are still known as the 'treasure caves'.

Beef Island, an island off Tortola's eastern end, has its own piracy legend. As the story goes, a widow who lived on the island grew tired of a band of ruffians raiding her herd of cattle. One evening she invited the group for dinner, and poisoned the lot, a fitting revenge. Jost Van Dyke and Bellamy Cay are two other islands named for the cutthroats who once frequented the area.

Until the late sixteenth century, Spain with its mighty armada had dominated the isles of the Caribbean. But as the maritime might of Spain weakened, other European nations began to enter the scene. One of the first successfully to challenge the Spanish in the Caribbean was the English adventurer, Sir Frances Drake. In 1594, the famed, but now ageing privateer put in at Virgin Gorda's North Sound to marshal and redistribute his troops before sailing on to San Juan, where he launched an unsuccessful attack against the Spanish fleet. The event, though, signalled the decline of Spain's supremacy in the Caribbean.

BRITAIN ENTERS THE SCENE

The strategic importance of the BVI in the seventeenth century began to increase as European nations vied for power through their expanding colonial empires. Among the first Europeans to settle on

◀ Traditional sailing ships still ply BVI waters

Tortola were the Dutch, who came to the island in the mid-1600s and established trading posts and fortifications. Their stay was short-lived. According to a Dutch account, in 1672, shortly after the outbreak of the Third Dutch War, the Dutch colonists requested that Colonel William Stapleton, who had been appointed Governor of the recently established English Colony of the Leeward Islands, take the island over for safe keeping during the war. Colonel Stapleton had a different story, claiming to have captured the island, and ordered the fort to be demolished and the 'Dutch Commissions' to be sent home.

Either way, in 1672 Tortola was in English control and administered by the Colony of the Leeward Islands. Tortola had no immediate economic value to the British, but they were still eager to hold on to this new territory as a way of solidifying their trading interests in the Caribbean and to secure British navigation throughout the area. In its early days, the BVI was, in part, settled by people of 'dubious character' and in 1724 a militia was established to control piracy and disreputable elements. The period also saw a few incursions by the Spanish, but these were soon quelled.

It was during this period that the Virgin Islands, which Columbus had seen as a single geographical unit, were divided between British and Danish islands. The Danish took formal possession of St Thomas in 1672, settled on St John in 1718 and purchased St Croix from the French in 1733. By 1735, the English had established sovereignty over not only Tortola, but also Virgin Gorda, Anegada and Jost Van Dyke.

Now that they were securely British, the islands of Tortola and Virgin Gorda were populated by an increasing number of English settlers, who carved large plantations out of the hillsides and low-lying areas and planted cotton and sugar cane. Distilleries were built and molasses and rum became the islands' most important products. Timber was also a valuable commodity in the Virgin Islands and a great deal of it was shipped off the islands in the early years of settlement.

Much of the rum that was produced was traded for African slaves whose forced labour soon became the basis of the islands' sugar economy. Compared to other West Indian islands, eking a living out of the Virgins' rocky soil was arduous, but as time went on the plantation economy became more prosperous. By 1751, Lieutenant-Governor James Purcell reported the production of one million pounds of cotton and one thousand casks of muscovado sugar. Sugar works, rum distilleries and great houses sprang up around the islands, built substantially of local stone, ballast bricks and coral. The walls of many of these once-proud edifices still dot the islands.

▲ Kegs of rum from the Cane Garden Bay Distillery

Along with increased prosperity and a growing population came calls for a constitutional government, and in 1773 the colony was granted its own legislature. It provided for a council of 12 members nominated by the Governor, and an assembly of eight representatives from Tortola, Virgin Gorda and Jost Van Dyke. Although the BVI had now been given control over its internal affairs, it was still far from autonomous. The territory remained under the jurisdiction of the Governor of the Leeward Islands, and the Crown had the power to approve and veto its laws. By now Tortola was becoming the economically dominant island and when the new assembly was formed it met in Tortola.

The eighteenth and nineteenth centuries were a turbulent era in Virgin Islands history. A series of wars, including the Napoleonic Wars from 1803 to 1815, were fought not only in Europe but in the New World as well. Most major European powers had Caribbean colonies which provided a major source of their wealth, and striking a blow at these colonies was often a way of inflicting a blow on the mother country.

To protect the British Virgin Islands, England constructed a series of forts along the coast of Tortola and shored up its militia. These included Fort Charlotte, which housed a substantial gun battery above

▲ Cannons once guarded the islands' plantations

Road Town, as well as Fort George and Fort Burt above the shores of Road Harbour. Forts Recovery and Purcell guarded Tortola's western access and Fort Hodge its eastern. Other fortifications on Virgin Gorda and some of the outer islands also guarded access to the territory. Even private plantations constructed gun emplacements to protect their vulnerable estates. The territory's defences were strengthened with the passing of the Powder Acts and Militia Acts. By 1801 over £36,000 had been spent on fortifications, a substantial sum for the time. Except for an incident when an American warship unsuccessfully threatened the territory during the American Revolution, the Virgin Islands never came under attack. Britain's naval might and increased patrols of the region were key factors in protecting the islands.

THE QUAKER INFLUENCE
One of the most influential and successful groups to live in the BVI were the Quakers, a peace-loving sect known for their outspoken anti-war and abolitionist views. Also known as the Society of Friends, the first Quakers came to the Caribbean in the late seventeenth century to escape persecution in England for their beliefs, which were considered highly controversial at a time of constant warfare and when the colonies depended on the slave trade for economic survival.

The first Quaker missionary to come to Tortola was Joshua Fielding, who held several meetings on the island. Among those impressed by his preaching was John Pickering, Lieutenant-Governor of Tortola. Pickering and other planters established their own meeting houses and in 1741 asked the Philadelphia Friends in the American colonies to send assistance. Opposition to the Friends in the BVI continued and Governor Pickering was eventually asked to resign because of his anti-war views. Nonetheless, the Quakers, who were among the islands' most successful planters, continued to flourish for another 40 years.

Three of the most well-known British Virgin Islands Quakers were Richard Humphreys, John Coakley Lettsom and William Thornton. Humphreys, an abolitionist and a supporter of education for African descendants, left the islands to live in Philadelphia, where he donated a considerable portion of his estate to 'the instruction of the African race in school learning in various branches of the mechanic arts and trades and in agriculture'. Founded in 1837, the school became the Institute for Colored Youth, and in 1921 it was taken over by the state of Pennsylvania. John Lettsom was born on Little Jost Van Dyke in 1744. He was sent to England for his education, eventually becoming the most distinguished physician of his day and founder of the London Medical Society, his crowning achievement. Lettsom was also the close friend of another eminent Virgin Islander, William Thornton.

Thornton, who was born on Tortola in 1761, is best known for designing the US Capitol building in Washington, DC. Like Lettsom, he went to England to study medicine, and following a brief stay in America, eventually returned to Tortola where he practised medicine, ran the family plantation and dabbled in architecture. In 1792, the American capital had recently been moved from Philadelphia to a swampy area on the Potomac River and Thomas Jefferson, then Secretary of State, advertised a competition to design a capitol building. Hearing of the competition while on Tortola, Thornton entered the contest. He sailed to America with what was to become the winning design, where he remained, becoming a well-known Washington architect and inventor, as well as the head of the first US Patent Office. Some of the remains of Thornton's Pleasant Valley estate can still be seen.

Although the Quakers' influence on the islands was great, it was brief, and by 1786, only a handful of Friends were left. Their spiritual commitment had been weakened by what they referred to as an 'over love of money' and the effects of slave holding.

SLAVERY COMES TO AN END

Slavery was the cornerstone of the BVI's plantation economy and without the importation of slaves from Africa, the vastly lucrative rum and sugar trade could not exist. As elsewhere in the Americas, slavery cast a dark shadow on BVI history. Slaves lived in huts of thatch, wattle and plaster; their food was meagre and their hours long. Keeping slaves docile and compliant was important to the smooth running of the territory and the slave population was kept under control through legislation and where possible, by denying them access to education. In the territory's first slave code which was passed in 1783, slaves were considered property and their owners were protected, as with any other property, against damage. It was a life of degradation and hardship and escape was difficult, although some slaves resorted to suicide and self-mutilation as the ultimate release. Not all slaves submitted meekly to their plight: there were slave revolts in 1790, 1823 and 1830, but all were unsuccessful.

With growing abolitionist sentiment in England and elsewhere, conditions began gradually to improve for the islands' slaves. A community of free Negroes was established at Kingston in 1833. The group which had been aboard a slave vessel were liberated following the abolition of the slave trade in 1807, eventually settling on Tortola where they were granted land at Kingston. As free Negroes they had the right to own a limited amount of land, as well as keep slaves.

It was the hanging of Arthur Hodge, a white planter long notorious for his cruel mistreatment of slaves, that best signalled changing times. In 1811, one of Hodge's slaves was fined for the crime of eating one of the planter's mangoes. When he couldn't come up with the money, he was severely whipped and eventually died. It was an act of cruelty that couldn't be condoned and the planter was tried and executed.

The voice of the abolitionist movement in England was finally heard on the first Monday of August, 1834, the day the Emancipation Proclamation was read out in the islands. The joyous occasion was celebrated throughout the islands with prayer ceremonies and picnics.

Life in the British Virgin Islands changed drastically with abolition. The islands' 5,000 slaves were now free men and women and although former slaves could earn 12 cents a day working in the fields, the plantation lifestyle was drawing to a close. A series of events, including a severe hurricane followed by a drought and a riot over the cattle tax, soon made the plantation system in the British Virgins untenable. By the 1850s most planters packed up and left, leaving the islands to their former slaves.

The plantation way of life was a relatively brief chapter in the story of the British Virgin Islands. The colony was among the last West Indian islands settled by the Europeans, and the first to be abandoned. For Virgin Islanders, one of the most important pieces of legislature to be passed during this period was the Encumbered Estates Act, which greatly simplified the sale of the islands' debt-ridden sugar plantations. Since the islands were now primarily inhabited by former slaves, property to a large part went into local ownership, giving British Virgin Islanders a sense of independence and pride not found elsewhere in the British Caribbean.

Land ownership though, did not make life in the British Virgin Islands easier for its people. Although Britain still ruled this distant colony, its interest in the area had waned. Services were minimal and the people settled into a routine of subsistence living. They fished, grew root crops and fruit, raised cattle and goats, traded with prospering St Thomas and on occasion earned extra income through smuggling goods onto the island.

THE PEOPLE HAVE A SAY

Throughout the late nineteenth and early twentieth centuries, British Virgin Islanders had little say in the running of their affairs, and this prompted residents occasionally to take matters into their own hands. One such disturbance occurred in 1890 when customs officers seized a boat for smuggling in order to avoid tax duties. Christopher Flemming, a resident of Long Look, emerged as a leader and is still regarded as a local hero for standing up to the government. After the commissioner fled to neighbouring St Thomas in order to rally aid, Flemming reportedly sat at the bureaucrat's desk, and although unable to read and write, cleared applicants through customs quickly – and without charging duty.

In 1901 matters took a turn for the worse when the Legislative Council was dissolved. Instead, the island was administered for the British Crown by the Governor of the Leeward Islands through a commissioner and an executive council that he appointed. As social services in the territory declined, British Virgin Islanders became increasingly resentful. Just before World War II, a petition was submitted to the Secretary of State for the Colonies requesting the reconstitution of the Legislative Council, but the war intervened and nothing came of this and another petition.

By 1947, there was renewed agitation for self-representation. One unlikely hero in the BVI's tale of self-determination was H. Faulkner, a fisherman from Anegada who came to Tortola with his pregnant

▲ The Road Town market circa 1960

wife. Following a disagreement with the medical officer over her care, he went to the marketplace in the centre of Road Town and for several nights running criticized the government with mounting passion. His grievances struck a chord with other BV Islanders and a movement was born. In 1949 over 1,500 people led by Faulkner, community leaders, I. G. Fonseca, C. L. DeCastro and others marched to the commissioner's office and presented him with a document outlining their grievances. It had taken almost half a century, but the people's voices were finally heard and in 1950 an elected Legislative Council was reinstituted with great fanfare.

Over the next few years, BV Islanders continued to seek a greater measure of self-rule, and in 1966, a new constitution was implemented. As an indication of their new status, the British Virgin Islands were now referred to as a territory and no longer as a colony. The territory's first Chief Minister was H. Lavity Stoutt, who was elected in 1967, and who is credited with helping to launch this sleepy territory into the modern world.

❹ The modern ages
Development and government

AN EMERGED NATION

Although the British Virgin Islands might be termed a developing nation by some, it hardly seems a fitting description for islands that have emerged from poverty and obscurity so rapidly. The BVI still has a few of the quaint trappings of a rural nation – old gents ride their donkeys along the Ridge Road, cows and goats wander the streets to the dismay of gardeners, and kids happily gnaw on stalks of sugar cane just as they did a hundred years ago. Yet, this is now a country with ADSL lines, satellite TV and a cell phone in every other pocket. The BVI has thriving financial and tourism industries and a government that is run with the help of computers and professional consultants.

Although ostensibly a British territory, the BVI has become an increasingly autonomous nation, controlled by a locally elected government. Modelled to a great extent on the British ministerial form of government, the BVI passes its own budget and determines its laws and social programmes. Like the British Prime Minister and cabinet, the territory's Chief Minister and ministers of the Executive Council are selected by the members of the majority party.

The Legislative Council is elected by the general populace from the territory's nine electoral districts. Four additional at-large representatives are also elected. Included in the Executive Council are the Chief Minister; the Minister for Natural Resources and Labour; the Minister for Communication and Works; the Minister for Education and Culture; and the Minister for Health and Welfare. Along with the Legislative Council, the Executive Council is responsible for setting the government's policies.

The Governor, who is appointed by Britain, is the Queen's personal representative and head of the Executive Council. He is also responsible for external affairs and internal security. The BVI also has its own judiciary, although the appeals court is a regional one, and the Queen's Privy Council acts as a final court of appeal.

AN ECONOMIC SUCCESS STORY

The formation of a modern government is only one part of the BVI's economic success story, a tale of rags to riches brought about by the development of both the tourism and financial services industries.

▲ Little Dix Bay Hotel on Virgin Gorda

▲ Boarding the barge to Beef Island in the early 1960s

The BVI's growth as a tourist destination began in the early 1960s. Up until then, its infrastructure was unable to support tourism on a large scale. People who visited the BVI in the early and mid-twentieth century were hardy souls who didn't mind a slow and uncomfortable ferry or cargo boat ride from St Thomas – or by the 1950s, when the first small planes flown by maverick pilots ventured here, a hair-raising landing onto an unpaved runway at Beef Island. And then once here, the adventure continued. To get from Beef Island to Tortola, pioneering spirits boarded a rope-towed barge that might be shared with a farmer transporting a couple of pigs and a goat.

Before the 1950s the territory's sole guest house of note was the Social Inn, a quaint West Indian hostelry on Main Street. The Guana Island Club run by a couple from Boston, and located on an island of the same name, was built in the 1930s of solid masonry that had to be brought up the island's steep hill by donkey. But by mid-century, a few hoteliers began to make their way here. Fort Burt was built in the early 1960s, followed by Treasure Isle Hotel, also in Road Town, and Long Bay on Tortola's northwestern shore. It was the building of Little Dix Bay Hotel in Virgin Gorda by the American philanthropist, Laurance Rockefeller, in the early 1960s that launched the BVI into the realm of tourism in a big way. If he had confidence in the BVI, others could too. Rockefeller built not only a hotel, but also an airport, ferry dock and yacht harbour, seriously underwriting the infrastructure of that small island.

Development on Tortola followed suit. The Royal Engineers, a party-loving and boisterous lot, arrived to pave the runway at Beef Island; a road along the shoreline from Road Town to West End was carved out of the mountains; and electricity was hooked up to the outermost communities of the island. Virgin Gorda also received power when an underwater cable was laid. The face of Road Town began to change as well. The outer fringes of Road Harbour were filled in so that the yards of houses and shops on Main Street were no longer on the shoreline, but instead backed onto a new waterfront road. More of the harbour was filled in for a commercial area called Wickhams Cay.

As a number of luxury resorts began to spring up around the islands, including Peter Island, Biras Creek, the Bitter End Yacht Club and a little later on, Necker Island, owned by Virgin Records magnate, Richard Branson, the BVI began to develop a reputation as an upmarket destination. 'Yes, we're different' was one of the territory's earliest slogans, as it strove to set itself apart from mass tourism markets.

▲ The Sunny Caribbee shop was once the Social Inn

SMOOTH SAILING

It was the arrival of the first charter boat companies that had the greatest impact on the territory's early tourism development. The BVI was a sailor's heaven. The area's sheltered waters, secluded anchorages and abundance of islands in close proximity made it ideal sailing territory. A sailor could lunch in one secluded harbour, pull up anchor and after just an hour or two's sail, light up the barbecue in yet another stunning harbour.

The first bareboat company in the BVI was begun by an enterprising British surgeon, who had come to the BVI in the early 1960s to take up the government surgical post. An avid sailor, he set up a fledgling bareboat company using his own and one other boat. As it turned out, the company, which chartered its yachts without a skipper, was ahead of its time, and a few years later, it folded. The pioneering enterprise, though, paved the way for other companies to enter the scene and by the early 1970s the BVI had developed into the world's largest bareboating centre.

Along with bareboat companies, of which there are now more than a dozen based in the territory, came the development of the crewed charter boat industry. Catering to less-experienced sailors,

Sailing down the Sir Francis Drake Channel ▶

or those who would just prefer to sit back and be pampered for a week or two, these luxury yachts, both sail and power, come with a full complement crew and specialize in gourmet food and personalized service. Today over 600 bare and crewed charter boats call the BVI home. Fortunately for the world's sailors, the British Virgin Islands offers such a rich and varied array of anchorages and sailing destinations that there's always somewhere new to discover and an adventure still to be had.

FINANCE TROPICAL-STYLE

Tourism and finance are not necessarily two industries that spring to mind as interrelated, but here in the BVI they go hand in hand: twin pillars which support the territory's economic growth. It can seem incongruous seeing sarong-clad and sun-bronzed tourists walking down the street alongside a group of accountants and lawyers in pin-striped shirts and ties, but the sight highlights exactly what sets the BVI apart. It's a Caribbean nation that capitalizes on its natural charms, but also has one of the region's highest standards of living.

The BVI's financial services sector was launched in the 1980s with the passing of the International Business Companies Ordinance (IBC) which exempted offshore companies from BVI income tax. The territory's stable government, its US dollar economy and a strict regulatory body have made the BVI one of the world's leading international finance centres.

The British Virgin Islands is a leader in IBC registries, and over half a million companies are on its registers. A system of incorporation by registration through a licensed registered agent in the BVI makes it possible for most companies to be operational within a day.

The finance services sector includes mutual fund administration. The BVI also specializes in insurance management and is a highly regarded jurisdiction. In addition, it offers trust formation, shipping registry and accountancy and legal services. The territory has been careful in the granting of banking licences and does not issue them lightly: only reputable institutions with a good track record can be eligible. To protect the BVI's reputation, it has passed anti-money-laundering legislation on the same model as that of the United Kingdom.

Investors, it seems, have the best of both worlds in the BVI: a domicile in which to incorporate a business, as well as a sun-drenched locale in which to work on a tan.

The BVI is home to one of the region's largest charter yacht flotillas ▶

⑤ Meeting the Virgins
An overview of the islands

TORTOLA, THE BIG ONE

Big in the British Virgin Islands is a relative term. All our islands are small and fairly simple to get around. At 17 miles long and 3 miles (27 by 5 km) wide, Tortola, the largest in the island chain, is about the same size as Manhattan, but with a much more modest population of just over 18,000. On Tortola though, our highrises are mountains, beautiful green-carpeted hillsides that can seem precipitously steep at times, but which create breathtaking vistas at almost every turn. Like a good penthouse apartment, there is virtually nowhere on Tortola that doesn't have a good view.

The highest point in the British Virgin Islands is on Sage Mountain which can be reached by driving along Tortola's dramatic Ridge Road.

▲ Long Bay on Tortola is one of the island's many stunning beaches

Along the ridge are some old-style West Indian buildings built of wood or masonry, and painted in terrific Caribbean colours, terraced farms planted with cassava and other root crops, and gardens of bougainvillea and frangipani.

At sea level, things are more down to earth. Tortola is the commercial centre of the BVI, and its main town, gradually becoming a small city, is Road Town. Road Town is the seat of BVI government, which is primarily housed in a three-storey glass and masonry building on the edge of the harbour. The territory's court house and Legislative Council chambers are in Road Town, as are the island's main shopping district, several marinas, hotels and dozens of offices for the territory's burgeoning financial industry (they're in the buildings with the imposing name plates and double barrelled names).

The island's north shore is where you will find the beaches: classic white sand beaches fringed with palms and seagrapes. Some, like Cane Garden Bay, are also the location of small communities; others, like the eastern end of Long Bay, are lined with a hotel and guest houses. But others are virtually empty expanses of sand which can only be reached by hiking down from the ridge, or by boat on a calm summer day.

VIRGIN GORDA, THE FAT ONE

The Spanish seafarer who named Virgin Gorda must have been at sea too long. As the story goes, he looked at the island's mountainous profile, and likening it to a voluptuous woman lying on her back, dubbed it Virgin Gorda, the Fat Virgin. Virgin Gorda is voluptuous, but in other ways. Its beaches are among the islands' most sumptuous and it is filled with an opulent array of flora, fauna and scenery.

Most visitors arrive by ferry in the Valley, an area of softly rolling hills and large granite boulders that are sprinkled through the countryside like a child's giant building blocks. Drier than other parts of Virgin Gorda, this area is filled with large cacti and a variety of water-conserving succulents. Also known as Spanish Town, the Valley was once a centre of sugar cultivation, and for a brief period in the early 1700s this small island of only 8 square miles (20 square kilometres) was more populous than Tortola.

The Valley is the island's commercial centre, although that is a relative term for this lightly populated island of just over 3,000 full-time residents. A small airport connects the island to Tortola and other Caribbean locations and there is a yacht harbour containing shops and restaurants. Luxury vacation accommodation, both resorts and villas, is spread along the north shore beaches and dots the Valley.

▲ An aerial view of Virgin Gorda, the 'Fat Virgin'

Virgin Gorda has two distinct areas, the Valley and North Sound. Connecting the two parts is a scenic road that crosses a narrow neck of land fringed by a sandy bay. The road forks either to the left where there are several beaches, hotels and resorts, or to the right where it climbs a steep mountain that is capped by Gorda Peak, the island's highest point. It then descends precipitously to the village of Gun Creek and the North Sound area, the location of several well-known island resorts.

JOST VAN DYKE, THE FUN ONE

Until very recent times this sparsely populated island of just 220 souls was a sleepy isle that seemed to have been bypassed by the modern world. There was no electricity, except for a generator or two, no telephones and the island's one road was the sandy track that ran along the beach front of Great Harbour. That's all changed now. There is a road leading up and over the hill to White Bay and another to Little Harbour on the island's east side. But don't expect a traffic jam, there are still only a few cars and taxis.

Great Harbour is the island's main bay and is where the daily ferry from the West End of Tortola docks – which unless you are on your own boat is the only way to get here. If you spend the night, and Great Harbour is a popular yacht anchorage, local bands can be heard

▲ Foxy Callwood entertains visitors to Jost Van Dyke

from several of the bars lining the bay's sandy beach. Great Harbour is also the home of Foxy, a charismatic island calypsonian, whose beach bar is located at the Bay's eastern end. It is the venue of a famous float-in New Year bash attended by thousands of yachtsmen that has been called one of the world's three best New Year's Eve parties (the other two are Times Square in New York City and Trafalgar Square in London).

To the west of Great Harbour is White Bay, a striking stretch of white sand. This bay is popular with day trip boats which bring people in to sunbathe on the beach and snorkel the reef just offshore. The Sandcastle Hotel and its infamous Soggy Dollar Bar are found here, along with several guest houses and other sand-in-your-toes watering holes. The Bay also has a watersports rental centre. Little Harbour, another popular, but quieter anchorage can be found to the east of Great Harbour. This sheltered inlet has a small marina and a few more beach bars offering West Indian food and island drinks. Diamond Cay, on the island's easternmost point which faces Little Jost Van Dyke, has another marina and restaurant.

ANEGADA, THE REMOTE ONE

For centuries this island, which lies about 40 miles (65 kilometres) north of Tortola, was largely isolated from the rest of the BVI. Few vessels dared venture near it, protected as it is by a treacherous reef that over the years has ensnared countless ships. The remains of vessels from Spanish galleons to twentieth-century refrigeration ships litter the sea bed. Sometimes known as the 'drowned island' because of its low-lying profile, Anegada is barely 28 feet (8.5 metres) at its highest point. The island is ringed by miles of powdery white sand that seem to stretch off into infinity. It has one small community called the Settlement and several inland salt ponds, which are the home of a growing flamingo population. Another of the island's distinctive residents is the Anegada iguana. You will have to be alert to spot one though. This impressive 5-foot (1.5-metre) long reptile has a shy nature and steely grey colouring that makes him blend into the island scrub.

Another distinctive feature of Anegada are the conch islands which lie just offshore on the south side. They are the accumulated shells of hundreds of years of conch fishing, piled high enough to form their own islets.

Anegada can be reached by plane or yacht – although some bareboat companies put the island off-limits because of the tricky entrance through the reef.

SANDY CAY, SANDY SPIT AND LITTLE JOST VAN DYKE

Located off the east coast of Jost Van Dyke, these islands are all uninhabited and popular anchorages for yachtsmen. Sandy Cay is one of the most spectacular isles in the chain. A proverbial desert island, small enough to walk around in less than an hour, it is fringed

▲ Sandy Spit

with immaculate white sand. At the centre there is a nature trail leading through palms and natural vegetation to the island's coral-strewn eastern side. Sandy Spit is even smaller and virtually all sand. There is good snorkelling on its outer reef. Little Jost Van Dyke was the birthplace of Dr John Lettsom, a well-known eighteenth-century London physician, and some of the remains of his family's plantation can still be found here. There are a couple of small beaches, on its southern side, and the energetic can walk over the top for a dramatic view of the Atlantic.

NORMAN ISLAND

A largely uninhabited island just to the south of Tortola, Norman has a colourful history of pirates and buried treasure. Local lore has it that Robert Louis Stevenson used Norman as the setting for his famed novel of cut-throat treachery, *Treasure Island*. It's easy to imagine the Bight, a deep and sheltered bay on the island's northwest end, as the perfect hideout for pirates stashing their loot. A series of small sea caves lie around the point just west of the Bight. These fascinating formations which contain shimmering orange and yellow soft corals,

▲ The Norman Island Caves are a popular port of call

▲ Processing salt on Norman Island

along with the reef that fringes the caves, are among the BVI's prime snorkelling spots. At the Bight, there is a beachside restaurant called Pirates, as well as the islands' only floating restaurant, the Willy T.

SALT ISLAND

Salt Island and its residents played an important role in Virgin Islands history. The location of several salt ponds, the island once provided passing ships and BVI residents with the salt needed for food preservation. Salt was so important to the way of life here that people throughout the territory would join Salt Islanders in the annual salt harvest. A time of both hard work and festivity, the harvesting would be preceded by a party that lasted well into the night. The following morning the opening, or the 'breaking of the pond', would be presided over by the territory's governor, a government agent and a contingent of the Royal BVI police force. Up until recently, one or two residents kept up the tradition of salt harvesting, but now the island is uninhabited. Along the island's west coast are the graves of some of the victims of the RMS *Rhone*, a mail packet ship that sank off Salt Island during a hurricane in 1867.

A FEW MORE ISLANDS

As the saying might go, 'There are so many islands and so little time.' One of the delights of the BVI is its seemingly infinite array of islands to visit. Although it's necessary to have a boat to reach most of them (not a problem in this charterboat capital) some, like Peter Island and Marina Cay, which are the sites of resorts and restaurants, provide a regular ferry service. Other well-known island resorts include Cooper, Guana, Necker and Little Thatch. In addition there are many uninhabited islands of interest to yachtsmen. These include Ginger Island, Great Thatch, the Dogs and Fallen Jerusalem.

⑤ Touring Tortola
Where to go and what to see

ROAD TOWN

The BVI is primarily comprised of small villages and rural settlements. Road Town is its only fully fledged town and although it's grown rapidly in recent years, it remains small enough to get around easily by foot. **Main Street** is the island's original main thoroughfare and commercial district. Today, the narrow one-way road contains a number of gift and apparel shops and art galleries, as well as several buildings of historical interest. A good place to start a walk is at the Sir Olva Georges Plaza, which with its shady trees, fountain and benches, serves as the community's town square. Across from the plaza is the **Post Office**, which was built in 1865. The colonnaded building once housed the government's main administrative offices, and some government offices still remain there, along with the philatelic bureau.

As you move east along Main Street, you will come to the **Virgin Islands Folk Museum**. This small museum is located in an early twentieth-century wooden building constructed in the traditional way with post and beam, a hip roof and a long, covered verandah. Inside there are relics from the RMS *Rhone*, a mail packet ship that sank in a hurricane in 1867, and artefacts from the Amerindian site at Belmont including domestic objects such as a spindle whorl for spinning cotton and

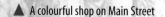
▲ A colourful shop on Main Street

▲ A panoramic view of Road Harbour

clay pots. There are also ceremonial pots and other religious objects dating from approximately 800 to 1000 AD. Other items of interest include pieces from the plantation era and a collection of photos of Tortola from the early twentieth century. The museum contains a small shop selling books and other items.

As you walk down the street you will see other examples of early West Indian buildings, although these wooden structures are gradually disappearing, victims of the ravages of time and a drive to modernize. Made of local hardwoods and featuring traditional hip roofs and cool porches, they were once the homes of prominent families and the premises of local businesses. The Sunny Caribbee building was once the **Social Inn** and just a bit further down the street you will come to the recently renovated **St George's Anglican Church**. The island's first Anglican Church was built in 1819. The original '**Her Majesty's Prison**', an imposing structure with thick white walls and a formidable arched gate, is next door. Just past the prison is the Methodist Church.

From Main Street cross over to the waterfront road and walk westward back towards the plaza. Just before the ferry dock on the harbour side of the road you will come to the **Crafts Alive** market, a charming collection of West Indian-style houses which contain a variety of craft shops and art galleries, as well as stores selling tee shirts, tropical clothing and other gift items. Laid out like a small park, the area is linked by neat grassy lawns and serpentine stone pathways.

The **Botanic Gardens** and **Old Government House** are two essential stops when visiting Road Town. Located on the town's eastern end, the gracefully landscaped Botanic Gardens contain a wide variety of tropical flora (see Chapter 8). Old Government House, the former residence of the British governors of the BVI, has been recently restored and is now open for tours. Located just west of Road Town's centre, it also contains a small museum (see Tortola's historic areas).

AROUND TORTOLA

Touring the remainder of Tortola is simple. There are only a few main roads and deciding which way to go is mostly a matter of choosing a clockwise or anti-clockwise direction. Along the way you will encounter a number of steep climbs and challenging switchbacks, but you will be rewarded by many spectacular views. (A road map,

▲ A view of the north shore including Carrot Bay, Apple Bay and Long Bay

▲ Soper's Hole Wharf and Marina

available at the BVI Tourist Board office in Road Town, or your rental car agency, will be helpful for this excursion.)

If you are starting in Road Town, head west towards **Soper's Hole** on the island's West End. The ride has to be one of the world's most enjoyable. The road hugs the coast and offers a diorama-like view of many Virgin Islands including Peter Island (with Dead Chest off its eastern end), Norman, the Indians, Flanagan (a small island claimed by both the BVI and the USVI) and St John (part of the USVI). In the distance towards the west you will see the western tip of St Thomas, another US Virgin Island.

Soper's Hole is the port of entry for yachts, and for ferries arriving from the US Virgin Islands. The ferry terminal, several restaurants and a car rental firm are located on the bay's Tortola side. Across the way on Frenchman's Cay (the two islands are connected by a short bridge) you will find the Soper's Hole Wharf and Marina, a charming and colourful shopping and marina complex designed in a traditional West Indian style. In addition to shops, the area contains offices and restaurants. A boatyard, a hotel and restaurants can also be found on Frenchman's Cay.

From Soper's Hole drive over Zion Hill to the scenic north shore road. Turn left at the bottom of Zion Hill and drive up the small hill that

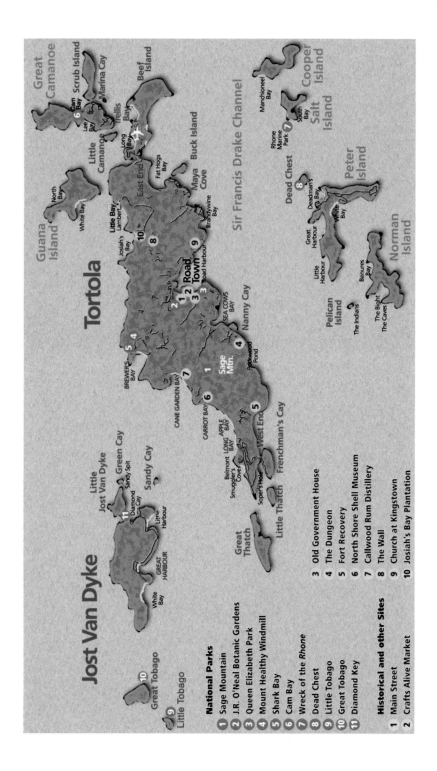

Jost Van Dyke

Tortola

Sir Francis Drake Channel

National Parks

1. Sage Mountain
2. J.R. O'Neal Botanic Gardens
3. Queen Elizabeth Park
4. Mount Healthy Windmill
5. Shark Bay
6. Cam Bay
7. Wreck of the *Rhone*
8. Dead Chest
9. Little Tobago
10. Great Tobago
11. Diamond Key

Historical and other Sites

1. Main Street
2. Crafts Alive Market
3. Old Government House
4. The Dungeon
5. Fort Recovery
6. North Shore Shell Museum
7. Callwood Rum Distillery
8. The Wall
9. Church at Kingstown
10. Josiah's Bay Plantation

separates Apple Bay and Long Bay; here you will be treated to one of the island's best beach views: **Long Bay's** almost mile long beach, fringed by a feathery palm grove and with the dramatic backdrop of Belmont Hill. The view is even better at sunset. The Long Bay Beach Resort and many guest houses are tucked behind the beach. As you drive back through **Apple Bay** you will pass Sebastian's and Sugar Mill hotels, several restaurants and the famous Bomba's Shack, known for its Full Moon parties, a monthly spectacle which draws people from throughout Tortola – as well as several neighbouring islands.

Carrot Bay is a charming village on Tortola's northwestern shore that is a centre for local fishermen, many of whom still launch their small fishing boats from the bay's shores. The village also contains a number of fine examples of traditional West Indian houses, and several restaurants specialize in local food. The North Shore Shell Museum, which is also a restaurant, contains an unusual assortment of cultural memorabilia and artefacts – plus lots of local shells.

Cane Garden Bay is at the centre of the BVI's lush and highly photogenic north shore. A semicircular bay, it is the location of a bustling village with several churches, a primary school and a few shops, as well as homes and guest houses on the beach and along its hillsides. If you like beach activities, or have children, you can rent a plethora of watersports equipment. The centuries-old Callwood Rum Distillery, at the back of the bay, is open to the public for tours and still sells its potent rum. For night owls, Quito's (run by well-known BVI singer Quito Rymer) and Myett's are among several hot spots that provide local entertainment.

Brewer's Bay is a lush bay with a small village and a quiet beach. The name attests to the area's heyday as a major sugar growing and rum production centre, and the ruins of one of its primary distilleries loom above the road on its eastern end. Above Brewer's on its eastern point is the Shark Bay National Park. Mount Healthy Windmill, also a national park, can be found on the hill above the Bay's eastern approach. (For more on both parks, see Chapter 8.)

One of Tortola's many scenic areas, the **Ridge Road** runs along the island's mountainous spine from Sage Mountain on its western end to Josiah's Bay to the east. From its lofty heights, there are sweeping views of the surrounding sea and islands, as well as glimpses of villages, terraced valleys and some of Tortola's less accessible bays.

The Ridge Road's best-known attraction is **Sage Mountain National Park**. This gem of a park is perfect for those who like to hike, but not too strenuously. The trails are gravelled and some of the

▲ The Wall, a series of murals depicting traditional BVI activities, is located on the Ridge Road

plants of this second growth forest are marked, making a walk here an interesting lesson in local flora. The beginning of the trail to the park is located along the western end of the Ridge Road. (For more about Sage Mountain, see Chapter 8.)

As you drive along the road through the central portion of the island, you will pass the **Wall**, a colourful mural depicting a series of historical and cultural scenes painted by local artists.

East End is actually a series of villages that includes Fat Hog's Bay, Long Look and Greenland. Hodges Creek, also at East End, contains a marina, hotel, and charter boat base.

As its name implies, cattle were once raised on **Beef Island**, which also contained an Amerindian village and was a popular hangout for the pirate Black Sam Bellamy. Today, it is the location of the Terrence B. Lettsome Airport and several guest houses. Trellis Bay, a large sheltered harbour, is a popular yachting anchorage. Art galleries, shops and restaurants can be found along the bay's shoreline. There is also a windsurfing firm and a cyber café. Although not part of Tortola, Beef Island is connected by a bridge, and residents treat the two islands like they are one and the same.

As you drive through the island try to take the time to meet some of the people along the way. Families have lived in these communities for generations. In Apple Bay there are Stoutts, Molyneux and Smiths. In Carrot Bay you are bound to meet members of the vast Donovan family and in Cane Garden Bay you will meet the Rhymers, Henleys and Callwoods. The Penn family is among the many families living at East End. Local legend has it that the East End Penns are descended from Richard Penn, the brother of the famous William. According to the quaint, but unsubstantiated story, the two Quaker brothers tossed a coin to see which one would head for the American colonies and which would go to Tortola. Chance had it that William went to America, where he founded Pennsylvania, while brother Richard sailed to Tortola.

TORTOLA'S HISTORIC AREAS

From an early twentieth-century governor's home to the remains of old forts and the tumble-down walls of eighteenth-century plantation houses, tantalizing remnants of history can be found throughout the islands. Some have been restored and are being used for new purposes, like the former sugar works that now house restaurant dining rooms at Sugar Mill and Long Bay hotels. Others are mere rubble walls, all that is left of a once vibrant era of rum and sugar production.

The **Callwood Rum Distillery**, at the back of Cane Garden Bay and towards its western end, is the islands' oldest functioning distillery. Owned by the Callwood family, the distillery, which has been in operation for over two centuries, offers a fascinating glimpse into the BVI's rum making tradition. Housed in its original stone plantation-era building, it is permeated with the musty aromas of centuries of rum production. Around the premises, one can see antiquated copper and iron boiling kettles, crushing machinery and the still, all of which continue to be used in the rum's production. Once distilled, the rum is stored inside oak barrels and is bottled and sold under the label Arundel Rum. For a small fee, visitors can take a short tour of the premises; bottles of the potent brew are also for sale.

Although not much of the original structure remains, the **distillery at Brewer's Bay** produced rum up until the mid-twentieth century. Located at the eastern end of the bay, and near the beach, the furnace now leans precariously over the road leading from the bay to the ridge. The boiling house and other parts of the ruin are partially concealed by foliage. Brewer's Bay was an important rum producing area in the eighteenth and nineteenth centuries and the remains of other sugar works are located within the valley.

Much of the estate that had been the **birth place of William Thornton**, a prominent BVI Quaker who went on to become the designer of the US Capitol building, has been destroyed or built

▲ The still at Callwood Rum Distillery

upon. Some stone walls and the foundations of a few of the estate buildings still remain though, and can be seen from the road leading to Pleasant Valley on Tortola's south shore about 5 miles (8 km) west of Road Town.

The **Anglican Church at Kingstown** highlights a fascinating event in British Virgin Islands history. Located about 3 miles (5 km) east of Road Town, the church was established in 1833 by a group of 600 free blacks who had been granted the land at Kingstown for a settlement. These freed slaves had been part of a group of 1,000 Africans being transported to the West Indies when the British slave trade was abolished in 1807. No longer slaves, the group was taken to Tortola where some were sent abroad for military service and the remainder were apprenticed to local planters and eventually set up a small community at what was called the 'African location at Kingstown'. All that remains of the village is the church, which is the property of the BVI Anglican Church. The roof to the building is long gone, but the stone walls are still standing although in need of further preservation. From time to time, services have been held inside this unique historic structure.

Josiah's Bay Plantation was a locally owned working rum distillery up until the 1940s, operating at full-tilt during the US Prohibition era when alcohol was illegal in the neighbouring US Virgin Islands. The Plantation which is located on Tortola's East End, just a short walk from Josiah's Bay beach, dates back to the eighteenth century. The building, which has been recently restored, houses a gallery, shop and a garden restaurant. Outside, the boiling vats, the still and the cane crusher are on display.

Fort Purcell, more commonly known as the **Dungeon**, was built around 1750 and named after James Purcell, the Governor of the Virgin Islands at that time. Constructed of stone and mortar, it was built to guard the Sir Francis Drake Channel from invasion from neighbouring St Thomas, St Croix and Puerto Rico. Much of the structure has been destroyed by time and neglect, but a stairway to a second floor, a munitions magazine, six gun emplacements on the building's front and two musketry platforms at the rear remain. There is a cell-like room on the first floor where crude drawings of a sailing ship, and a woman and soldier in eighteenth-century dress are etched into the wall, perhaps drawn by a prisoner passing the time away. The Dungeon is located just off the Sir Francis Drake Highway about halfway between Road Town and West End.

▲ The Dungeon was one of many forts that once protected the islands

In the eighteenth and early nineteenth centuries, defending the BVI against invasion by hostile nations had become a priority and a series of fortifications was constructed along the islands' coastlines and on strategically located promontories. Although the remains of many of these forts lie on private property, they are an important reminder of the BVI's turbulent history. At **Fort Recovery**, which is now the site of a hotel on Tortola's West End, there is a well-preserved tower. The commanding structure may have been constructed by the Dutch, who were among the island's first settlers, arriving here in the mid-seventeenth century. **Fort Burt** is the site of a hotel, which was built upon the original fort's foundations. Located on a hill on the western end of Road Town, the fort was well situated, offering troops a sweeping view of the entrance to the harbour. Cannons and a well-preserved magazine can still be seen on the grounds. When the grounds of the Old Government House were being excavated for the new Governor's residence next door, the stone walls of a Road Town fort were uncovered. These walls can be seen from the gardens at the back of the Old Government House Museum as well as from the reception area in the new Governor's residence, although this part of the premises is not open to the general public.

Old Government House is a historical home constructed in 1926, which was once the residence of the territory's governors. It sits on a

▲ Old Government House

knoll at the western end of Road Harbour and offers a commanding view of the Harbour and Road Town. Built with thick masonry walls to withstand hurricanes (the former Government House on that site was destroyed by a hurricane in 1924), the structure has heavy wooden shutters, a graceful entranceway, arched porticoes and a large, meandering garden. It is furnished with nineteenth- and early twentieth-century items that give it the 'lived in look' of a working Government House.

The home, which has been the site of several royal visits including those by Queen Elizabeth in 1966 and 1977, also contains a gift shop and a small museum housing mementos (including a guest book signed by the late Queen Mother) and artefacts from the early BVI. Also on display is a fascinating account of the hurricane that destroyed the original Government House, written by the then Governor's wife. During the storm, she and her children took shelter in the room that now contains the museum. The home and its gardens are open for tours from 9 am to 2 pm, Monday to Saturday. Next door to Old Government House and linked to it by a reception hall and patio is the current residence of the Governor of the British Virgin Islands.

GOING TO THE BEACH ON TORTOLA

The BVI has first class beaches. The water is invariably calm and crystal clear, and our white, powdery sand feels great between the toes. When going to the beach here, it's not a matter of deciding which beach to visit, but finding the time to visit them all. Most of the island's best swimming beaches hug the north shore. From west to east, here are some of the most popular.

The westernmost beach on Tortola is **Smuggler's Cove**, a lovely semicircular beach near Belmont. Fringed with coconut palms and sea grapes, it also has a good snorkelling reef just off the shore. Smugglers can get a bit crowded in season, but in the BVI, crowded is a relative term; wherever you go, there's always plenty of room to spread out a beach towel.

If you like leisurely scenic walks, **Long Bay**, a nearly mile-long beach at West End, is the perfect location. This long swath of pure white sand is good for sunbathing, and in the winter when there is a northern swell, the sea is ideal for body surfing. The beach has two distinct parts. At the eastern end, there is a hotel and guest houses set behind an arbour of seagrape and almond trees. The western section, which has a vast palm grove tucked in at the back, is more quiet. The beach offers little shade though, so take care if you have a tendency to burn.

▲ The tyre swing on Cane Garden Bay

The surf may not be as big as Hawaii's, but **Apple Bay** attracts surfers from around the world when there's a north shore swell during the winter months. Apple Bay is actually three bays in one: Apple Bay, Little Apple Bay and Capoons Bay. This unusual geographical fact is understood by the area's residents, although it mystifies others.

There is always something to do in **Cane Garden Bay**. This busy beach is sheltered by an extensive reef, which makes it calm for swimming most of the year, and it's also a popular anchorage. The sand is white and fine, ideal for building sand castles or running your toes through. There are several water sports firms renting out pedal boats, surf bikes, kayaks and floats, making the bay a good spot to bring children. An eclectic array of beach bars and restaurants is also a draw for yachtsmen, who make the sheltered anchorage a regular port-of-call.

The beach at **Brewer's Bay** borders a quiet canopy of tropical foliage. The sand isn't the island's whitest, but the water is calm and clear for a good part of the year. There is a campground at the back of the bay and the beach is often populated with enthusiastic campers, some of whom spend the entire winter lodged amongst the seagrapes. There are two beach bars on the bay for those in need of refreshment. The beach can be reached from the Ridge Road, or from Soldier Hill, which runs along the eastern ridge above Cane Garden Bay.

▲ The beach at Brewer's Bay

Brandywine Bay is a man-made beach, but with such good-quality sand, it's hard to tell. It's also the south shore's only beach and since it's just about 3 or 4 miles (5 km) east of Road Town it's easy to get to. Brandywine Bay is well sheltered, making this a good swimming area. For more privacy, stay at the western end.

Josiah's Bay at East End on the north shore is a dramatic beach with a great expanse of sand to recline on for sunning. It is popular with surfers, who enjoy riding the winter waves, and with young people who spend the afternoon with coolboxes and picnics, although if you'd rather not bring your own food, a beach bar serves burgers, fries and drinks. The beach has a few palm-frond sun shelters, but other than that, there's not much shade. To get here from Road Town, go east along the coast road and take the first left-hand turning after the police station.

Lambert Bay and **Little Bay** are at the easternmost end of Tortola. Lambert's sumptuous beach is long and wide with a resort and restaurant tucked into the valley behind. Little Bay, which requires a four-wheel drive vehicle to trek down a rutted road, has large boulders at each end and a lovely patch of sand for sunbathing. To get to these beaches from Road Town, go east along the coast road, take the second turning after the police station and follow it to the top and turn right.

Beef Island has several good beaches, all of which are calm year-round. The most impressive is **Long Bay**, which has a long sweep of semicircular sand. Its placid warm waters and long stretch of beach make this a popular picnic spot. It lies just past the bridge to Beef Island and is reached by a dirt road at the eastern end of the salt pond that lies at the back of the beach. **Well Bay** is a small beach on the island's southwestern point. The road, which is unpaved, but not rough, is the first one to the right after crossing the bridge. **Trellis Bay** is past the airport. It has a narrow strip of sand around its curving perimeter and a couple of beach bars, several shops, windsurfer and kayak rentals, as well as a cyber café in case you want to stay connected whilst enjoying the sun.

It's worth noting that the undertow on north shore beaches during a winter ground sea can be dangerous. Fortunately for water lovers, when one beach is out of action there are still plenty of others that are protected by coral reefs or are buffered by outer islands, making it a rare day when you can't enjoy the water. All beaches are open to the public to the high water mark.

⑦ Visiting Virgin Gorda and the other islands

Where to go and what to see

Virgin Gorda is smaller than Tortola and easy to get around. The Valley area, the western section of this fat virgin, is low-lying with gentle hills peppered with large boulders. If you like to hike, you can stride from the Virgin Gorda Yacht Harbour area to The Baths, Spring Bay or the Coppermine fairly readily. For most day trippers with time constraints, though, it is quicker and easier to take a taxi. To take in the whole island, it is best to rent a car.

VIRGIN GORDA: THE VALLEY

The **Virgin Gorda Yacht Harbour** is the main shopping area of the island, where you will find restaurants, clothing boutiques, gift shops,

▲ The Virgin Gorda Yacht Harbour

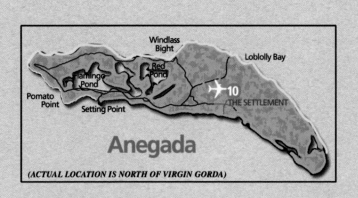

Windlass
Bight

Red
Pond

Loblolly Bay

Flamingo
Pond

Pomato
Point

Setting Point

THE SETTLEMENT

Anegada

(ACTUAL LOCATION IS NORTH OF VIRGIN GORDA)

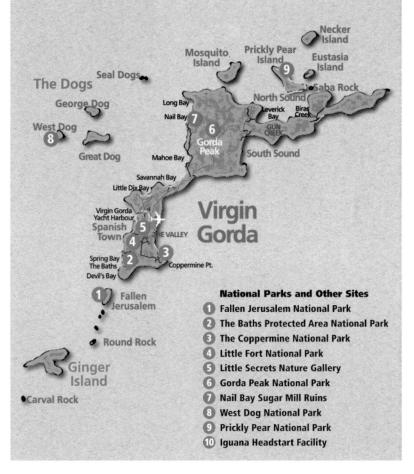

Necker
Island

Mosquito
Island

Prickly Pear
Island

Eustasia
Island

Seal Dogs

The Dogs

George Dog

Long Bay

Nail Bay

North Sound

Leverick
Bay

Biras
Creek

Saba Rock

West Dog

8

7

6
Gorda
Peak

GUN
CREEK

South Sound

Great Dog

Mahoe Bay

Savannah Bay

Little Dix Bay

Virgin Gorda
Yacht Harbour

Spanish
Town

5

4

THE VALLEY

**Virgin
Gorda**

Spring Bay
The Baths

Devil's Bay

2

3

Coppermine Pt.

1 Fallen
Jerusalem

Round Rock

**Ginger
Island**

Carval Rock

National Parks and Other Sites

1 Fallen Jerusalem National Park
2 The Baths Protected Area National Park
3 The Coppermine National Park
4 Little Fort National Park
5 Little Secrets Nature Gallery
6 Gorda Peak National Park
7 Nail Bay Sugar Mill Ruins
8 West Dog National Park
9 Prickly Pear National Park
10 Iguana Headstart Facility

a bank, bakery and dive shop, among other businesses. There is also a grocery store for provisions. Most of the businesses are located in a small shopping area centred on a landscaped courtyard. Others overlook the Yacht Harbour docks, which are lined with a copious display of sail and power boats.

Top of The Baths is a shopping area adjacent to the trail leading to Devil's Bay and The Baths from the Valley. It has a restaurant with a pool that is available to guests lunching there, and several small stores with island mementos and tropical fashions.

The Baths are Virgin Gorda's best-known tourist attraction. These famous boulders and the sea pools that they enclose have been called one of the world's natural wonders. (For more about The Baths, see Chapter 8).

Little Fort is yet another Virgin Gorda National Park. A nature reserve located to the north of Spring Bay, it also contains a small historic ruin.

The **Coppermine National Park**, which is located on a bluff on Virgin Gorda's southeastern peninsula, contains the ruins of a nineteenth-century mine operated by Cornish miners (see Chapter 8).

There is an 18-hole **miniature golf course** at the Mine Shaft Restaurant, located on Coppermine Road – an easy way to get in a quick round.

Other areas of interest in the Valley include St Ursula's Catholic Church, which is a significant landmark atop a knoll above the Yacht Harbour. St Mary's Anglican Church, the Methodist Church and several other churches are scattered throughout the Valley as well. The Valley is not a shopping mecca, but most essentials can be found on Virgin Gorda. Along Crab Hill Road you will find a few more businesses including the electricity corporation and a hardware store, and Flax Plaza has a shop, restaurant and hair salon. The Valley is also home to Little Dix Bay Hotel, Fisher's Cove Hotel and Olde Yard Village.

FURTHER AFIELD ON VIRGIN GORDA

The ruins of an eighteenth-century sugar mill can be found in the grounds of the **Nail Bay Resort** which is located along the coast road that hugs the north shore past Savannah Bay.

Leverick Bay borders North Sound, and can be reached by the road that winds past Gorda Peak. The Leverick Bay Hotel is here, as

◀ Virgin Gorda's dramatic coastline

well as many rental villas and several shops. There is a small beach and a pool at the restaurant.

Gun Creek is a small village on the southern shore of North Sound. The road to Gun Creek is steep and narrow, but affords lovely views of the village below and surrounding hillsides. On a clear day you will even be able to make out Anegada in the distant north. A dock at Gun Creek services ferries to elsewhere in the North Sound.

North Sound has sometimes been called the playground of the BVI. The Sound, which is located off Virgin Gorda's northern tip, is one of the BVI's largest and most sheltered anchorages. Here you will find the luxury resorts of Biras Creek and the Bitter End Yacht Club. **Saba Rock** is an island off the Bitter End where there is a small hotel, restaurant and a museum containing marine artefacts as well as items from the shipwreck of the *Atocha*.

Gorda Peak is Virgin Gorda's highest point and one of its many national parks. The walk up isn't overly strenuous and once at the top, there is a lookout with panoramic views of surrounding islands, which is well worth the trip. (For more details, see Chapter 8.)

GOING TO THE BEACH ON VIRGIN GORDA

On a scale of one to ten, three outstanding beaches score a resounding ten: **The Baths**, **Devil's Bay** and **Spring Bay**. Here beachgoers can have the best of all worlds: some of the BVI's most beautiful stretches

▲ Arriving at The Baths

of sand to sun on and those great big boulders that dominate the Virgin Gorda Valley landscape to both scale and admire. The only drawback to the area, especially The Baths itself, is that it can get busy when day charter boats anchor offshore, generally around midday. To enjoy the area at its best, come earlier in the day or later in the afternoon.

Because these beaches are part of the National Parks Protected Area, access is easy. A car park is located on a small hill just above the Area; here there is a map showing a trail to The Baths and one to nearby Devil's Bay. The easy-to-walk paths will take you past local vegetation, including cacti, wild frangipani, white cedars and pitch apple trees. The beach at The Baths is comprised of small stretches of sand shaded by those spectacular boulders, and both Devil's Bay and The Baths offer good snorkelling along the rocky shoreline. It is also possible to get between The Baths and Devil's Bay through the grottoes and labyrinthine passageways formed by the granite boulders. Even though ladders and ropes have been installed here and there to help would-be rock climbers, it's best to be agile before attempting the route.

Neighbouring Spring Bay is most easily reached by road, since the boulder route is an arduous and tricky climb. Spring Bay is just a mile or two east of The Baths, and its road, which is bordered by the gardens of several villas in the area, ends at this picture-postcard pretty beach. Like the Baths, Spring Bay is sprinkled with granite boulders made for climbing.

Valley Trunk Bay is yet another BVI beach where nature outdid itself. Wide and long, with marvellous pure white sand, the beach is bordered by a private estate and a palm grove. It is just east of Spring Bay and can be reached by boat when the sea is calm, or if you're feeling adventurous, along a rough path from Spring Bay.

Savannah Bay is a sun lover's beach and if you're seeking shade, look elsewhere. Instead, this lanky stretch of sand is ideal for an unhurried stroll, and its calm water is made for long, languid floats. It can be found along the narrow neck of land that links the Valley to the island's mountainous central portion.

To reach the beaches at **Mahoe Bay**, **Mountain Trunk** and **Long Bay**, take the road past Savannah Bay and go to the left, instead of up over the mountain towards North Sound. Mahoe Bay is a lovely beach bordered by a couple of small hotels including the Mango Bay Resort and Paradise Beach Resort, and several holiday villas. A restaurant is tucked beneath the point at the bay's western end. Nail

▲ Valley Trunk Bay on Virgin Gorda

Bay and Diamond Bay are part of the Nail Bay Resort and lie just to the east of Mahoe Bay. These beaches offer good sunning and reefs for snorkelling.

The resorts lining the **North Sound** have their own beaches including Leverick Bay, the Bitter End Yacht Club and Biras Creek. It's always fun to follow lunch at one of these popular resorts with a swim and a sunbathe.

PETER ISLAND

Deadman's Bay is an opulent white sand beach on the north shore of Peter Island, which is in large part owned by the Peter Island Resort. There is a ferry from Road Town for hotel guests, while yachtsmen tend to anchor off the quieter, western end of the beach. At the westernmost part of Deadman's Bay there is a nature trail, and another path at this end leads up to a small group of stone walls, once part of a sugar plantation. **White Bay** is on the island's south side and has a sweep of semicircular sand and some palm-frond sun shades; unlike Deadman's Bay which can have a bit of a surf in winter, it's generally calm. One can get here by a strenuous hike over the top of the island; better to have a boat and sail over. **Great Harbour** is also on the north shore. There's a compact beach and a beach bar

▲ Beautiful White Bay is two beaches in one

and restaurant, as well as watersports equipment, including kayaks, for rent. **Little Harbour** to the west has a small beach area with coarse sand, but the bay is quiet, and snorkelling the sea grass bed is wonderful.

JOST VAN DYKE

Great Harbour is both a village and a beach. This horseshoe-shaped bay is fringed with homes, beach bars and a church. Because the u-shaped bay is so sheltered, the water is calm here all the time. This is also a popular overnight anchorage, and the bay tends to come alive at night when the boats drop anchor just before sunset. One of the BVI's most beautiful beaches is **White Bay** on the western side of Jost Van Dyke. The beach is long with smooth white sand and has several beach bars along the way for shelter and sustenance. There are two sections to the beach, linked by an outcrop of rocks that has a path over the top, so it's almost like getting two beaches in one. There is good snorkelling offshore and the bay is generally calm enough to swim year-round. This is a popular beach with day-trip excursions from St Thomas, and during the middle of the day, the beach can get fairly full. But if you're looking for activity, this is a good place to go, especially since there is a watersports concession at the far end.

Sandy Cay and Sandy Spit are both small islands off the eastern tip of Jost Van Dyke which are fringed in luxurious swathes of sand. These are desert islands *par excellence* and should be visited by all serious beach aficionados.

BEACHES ON OTHER ISLANDS

Cooper Island has a beach bar and hotel located on Manchioneel Bay on the island's north shore, and of course, a beach. The bay is a popular port of call for cruising yachtsmen, and although it's not the BVI's whitest or most powdery beach, the water is calm and there are plenty of palm trees for shade. The bottom is grassy and if you're lucky you might see a sea turtle or two if you put on your mask and snorkel. Marina Cay, a small island with a resort and restaurant (Pusser's Marina Cay), has a nice little beach that offers snorkelling offshore. The Norman Island Bight has a small beach with beach chairs at Pirates, a waterfront bar and restaurant; offshore, a floating restaurant, the *Willy T*, provides more refreshments. Around the corner, Benure's Bay offers a bit of a rocky beach, but the real reason to go here is for the snorkelling.

▲ A young boy plays on one of Anegada's infinite beaches

Anegada has been called the 'beach lover's island' and for good reason. Start walking westward along the beach at Loblolly Bay, for instance, and you will feel as if there is no end in sight. And there pretty much isn't, since most of this unique coral atoll is ringed by sandy beach. Even the most die-hard beach lover just might get his fill here. Another interesting sandy stopover is Anegada Reef Hotel, where you can have a lobster lunch and a swim. Neptune's Treasure also specializes in fresh-caught fish and lobster and has a beach as well – this is Anegada after all. Windlass Point is a windswept beach where you might prefer to walk rather than swim, at least in the summer. Nurse sharks, a harmless variety that hug the sea floor, come here to give birth around August; watching them swim along the shore's edge is a fascinating pastime.

❽ From shipwrecks to rain forests

The BVI's diverse national parks

As island nations go, the British Virgin Islands is more fortunate than most. It is blessed with the obvious attributes: year-round sunshine, clear warm waters and sparkling white beaches. But what sets it apart from so many Caribbean nations is the diversity of its national parks.

When Laurence Rockefeller donated 92 acres on the top of Sage Mountain for the territory's first national park, the BVI set out on a course that has made it one of the Caribbean's most environmentally conscious countries. Today, the British Virgin Islands manages 20 national parks, including 18 land-based and one marine national park, which range in a dazzling display of diversity from the Wreck of the RMS *Rhone* to the spectacular Virgin Gorda Baths. There are the J. R. O'Neal Botanic Gardens, the eighteenth-century Mount Healthy Windmill and entire islands like West Dog and Little Tobago, which are bird sanctuaries. From the untamed to the pristine, each of the parks has its own distinct personality and its own special beauty.

The islands' parks take small slices of the BVI and show us how they once were. At Sage Mountain National Park, we can see the islands as they were prior to the plantation era when large trees, including mahoganies and other tropical hardwoods, covered much of Tortola's hillsides. Once colonized, large portions of the island were cleared for timber and to create crop land, and much, although not all, of what we see at Sage Mountain National Park is second growth. Fortunately in the island's incubating climate, it doesn't take long for renewal to take place, and while walking through the park with its abundant plant life, we can imagine an earlier era when the islands were still virgin.

The Mount Healthy Windmill, above Brewer's Bay, transports us to the eighteenth century, when sugar cane lined Tortola's hillsides and rum production made planters wealthy. The windmill was unique on Tortola, since even on these breezy islands, wind-generated power was unreliable and most planters preferred animal-drawn mill rounds to crush their cane.

The J. R. O'Neal Botanic Gardens ▶

The underwater remains of the RMS *Rhone* at the Wreck of the Rhone Marine Park put the focus on another chapter of BVI history. The wreckage of this vessel that sank in a mid-nineteenth century hurricane is a reminder of the destructive forces of nature, as well as a fascinating glimpse into the era of steam packet ships.

Other parks highlight our natural wonders. Who could stand beneath the massive boulders at The Baths and not marvel at the awesome geological forces that created them? Several years ago, scientists from Kew Gardens in London studied the flora and fauna of Gorda Peak on Virgin Gorda. What they found was an unbelievably rich diversity of plant and animal life. They discovered new species and noted others that were endangered.

Ultimately all of our parks are guardians of the territory's irreplaceable treasures. The BVI's national parks not only evoke our sense of history and give us a greater appreciation of its natural environment; they also preserve what was so beautiful in the past, so that it will remain that way in the future.

A brief description of the BVI's national parks follows, but the only way truly to appreciate our parks is to discover them for yourself.

TORTOLA'S PARKS

Lush and green with hanging vines, gargantuan elephant ears and bountiful ferns, **Sage Mountain National Park** is not exactly the Amazon rain forest, but it does exhibit many of its luxuriant characteristics. The northeast section of the mountain receives more rainfall than other areas of the territory because of its elevation (at 1,716 feet, 523 metres, the mountain is located at the BVI's highest point) and the direction of the prevailing winds. The southern slopes are much drier and are representative of Caribbean dry forest habitats. The difference between the two sides can be seen as you cross the ridge from the northern to the central trail.

The park has several paths, all gravelled to make traversing them easier. The Mahogany Forest Trail leads to the park's highest point through a grove of West Indian broadleaf mahoganies. The Rain Forest Trail and the Henry Adams Loop lead down to the lushest and most primordial section of the park. Dark and damp with a thick carpet of moss covering boulders and patches of rich soil, the loop contains a canopy formed by the park's largest trees. Among these giants are a 100-foot (30-metre) bulletwood whose trunk is 4 feet (1.2 metres) in diameter and the ficus, which produces large aerial roots often extending from the branches to the ground.

▲ A view from Sage Mountain

The **J. R. O'Neal Botanic Garden** is located at the back of Road Town near the police station, a calm oasis in the midst of this bustling town. The park, which is managed by the National Parks Trust, covers 2.8 acres, small enough to get around easily in an hour or two, but large enough to contain a cornucopia of indigenous and exotic tropical plants, many of which were introduced by the Caribbean's earliest settlers. Among others are hybrid hibiscus in a stunning medley of colours, bromeliads, cacti and a wide variety of ferns. Paths shaded by graceful arbours meander through the garden, and park benches are scattered in strategic spots on its lawns. The centrepiece of the garden is a graceful Victorian-style fountain surrounded by wooden benches. Other attractions include an orchid pavilion, pergola walk, lily pond, waterfall, tropical bird houses and a miniature rain forest. There is also a medicinal herb garden which features a fascinating array of local plants used as traditional remedies. The gardens are named after J. R. O'Neal, a prominent BVI businessman who was instrumental in the development of the BVI's national parks system.

If you are walking through Road Town and have already been to Government House, stroll just a little further west and you will come to the **Queen Elizabeth II Park**. This peaceful refuge covers less than an acre, but it is lined with the islands' national tree, the White Cedar, and offers an ideal vantage point for viewing the yachts that sail in and out of Road Harbour. The park, which is managed by the National Parks Trust, has benches so you can rest your weary feet, a picnic area and a children's playground.

The late eighteenth-century **Mount Healthy Windmill** overlooks a valley above Brewer's Bay. The structure was built by Bezaliel Hodge prior to 1780, but upon his death was taken over by the island's largest landowner, James Anderson. The power generated by the windmill was used to operate a crusher to extract juice from the sugar cane that was grown on the surrounding hillsides. The juice ran down a sluice connected to a sugar production factory where it was boiled in a series of vats (or coppers as they were called) until sugar crystals were formed. This small park (just under an acre in size) enjoys cool breezes because of its lofty position, and pastoral views. There are also picnic tables, and a short, easy to negotiate nature trail. Nearby are the remains of the boiling house, storage room, cistern and stables which are best viewed from the road since they are located on private property.

Shark Bay is a national park and nature reserve located above the eastern end of Brewer's Bay. It features a dramatic trail to Anderson Point, the bay's furthest promontory, and offers several windswept views of the sea and Tortola's craggy north shore along the way. Although the trail is not steep, it is rocky and not always easy going.

The Mount Healthy Windmill ▶

If you're looking for an easy stroll, it's better to stick to the Botanic Gardens. A few ladders have been constructed along the way to help negotiate some of the larger boulders. About mid-way along the walk, the trail forks, with one path leading across the ridge above Brewer's Bay, just short of Anderson Point. The other trail leads to the 'Bat Cave', an enormous rock formation with an impressive dome-shaped roof. It will have you speculating on the geological forces that created such a structure.

VIRGIN GORDA'S NATIONAL PARKS

The Baths Protected Area is the most well-known attraction in Virgin Gorda, and probably the entire BVI. This series of awe-inspiring

▲ One of the sea pools at the Virgin Gorda Baths

boulders perched helter-skelter atop one another along the sea's edge is a work of natural art. You have to climb inside the grottoes formed by the boulders to appreciate them fully. Shallow sea pools and the ethereal shafts of light coming from above create the feel of a cathedral vault. Etched by the weather and flecked with algae in different hues, some of the boulders look more like a modern sculpture than a geological formation. A series of wooden ladders helps visitors negotiate the giant rocks and eventually leads to the neighbouring beach, Devil's Bay.

Devil's Bay, located just southwest of The Baths, is a gorgeous stretch of powdery white sand. It is also sprinkled with giant boulders, although less profusely. Snorkellers will enjoy exploring the area's rocky perimeter, and if the sea is calm and you are a good swimmer, you can snorkel to The Baths.

Spring Bay has clear blue waters, bright white sand and a few large boulders. If you dream of an idyllic beach where you can swim and sunbathe, you can't do much better than Spring Bay.

The Baths, Devil's Bay and Spring Bay are known as The Baths Protected Area. Both The Baths and Devil's Bay can be reached either by boat from the shore or by trails leading from a car park in the Valley. Spring Bay is reached by a separate road just to the northeast of the Baths.

Little Fort is also a national park with Bath-like boulders scattered along its interior. The park's point is the site of a small fortification and some masonry ruins including a munitions store. Much of the area, which is a nature reserve, is inaccessible.

The **Coppermine**, a cluster of partially standing stone buildings on a windswept bluff, is all that remains of a singular chapter in BVI history. From 1839 to 1842, a company of St Thomas businessmen were granted a licence to mine copper, but the price of copper dropped the next year, forcing the company out of business. A Cornish company reopened the mine in 1859, and in 1862 exported over £10,000 pounds of ore; unfortunately the vein was soon depleted and the mine once again closed.

Today, the mine's crushing plant with its tall stone chimney still dominates the site. The building housed the steam engine which had been used to pump water out of the primary shaft, extract the ore and crush it for shipping. The site contains at least seven underground shafts 15 to 200 feet (4.5 to 61 metres) deep, which visitors should be careful to avoid. The Cornish miners may not have been the first to mine the site though. Local lore has it that the Spanish had observed

▲ The Coppermine

Indians wearing 'gold' jewellery when they passed through the Virgin Islands, and some believe that the Spanish may have mined copper there briefly as well. The mine, which is located on the southwestern point of Virgin Gorda, can be easily reached from the Valley along Coppermine Road.

Gorda Peak, a 265-acre dry forest rich in biodiversity, is one of the gems of the BVI national parks system. The park is located at the centre of the island at the 1,000-foot (305-metre) point and continues up to 1,370 feet (417 metres), the highest point on Virgin Gorda. Gorda Peak is representative of Caribbean dry forest habitat and is home to several endemic and endangered species of animals and plants. Along the walk to the top, you will see a wide variety of native plants including bromeliads and six species of native orchids. Several types of birds make the park their home, as do a variety of lizards, including the world's smallest, the Virgin Gorda gecko. Other animals found in the park include native tree frogs, which can be identified by their bird-like chirping sound, soldier crabs and small (harmless) snakes. At the top of the park is an observation platform which offers a spectacular panoramic view of many of the Virgin Islands, including North Sound and Anegada. On a clear day, St Croix, which is more than 50 miles (80 km) to the southeast, can be seen in the distance.

MORE BVI NATIONAL PARKS

The BVI has many areas to explore by boat. If you're chartering by the week, it's easy to venture to these out of the way places. But if you're not, the best way to explore some of these less accessible gems is to rent a power boat for the day. On a calm day, nowhere in these closely knit islands is out of reach.

The **Wreck of the RMS *Rhone* Marine Park** is the BVI National Parks Trust's only underwater park. Teeming with fish life and encrusted with colourful corals, the RMS *Rhone* is on the 'must do' list of most divers visiting the British Virgin Islands. Dashed against the rocks off the southwest shore of Salt Island during the hurricane of 1867, the 310-foot (94-metre) mail ship foundered and sank quickly; only 23 of the 147 crew and passengers aboard survived. The vessel's remains are extensive and have become a haven for an infinite variety of marine creatures including corals, sponges, parrot fish, wrasse, grouper and angel fish. The wreck, which broke in half while sinking, lies in 20 feet (6 metres) at the shallowest (making it accessible to snorkellers as well as divers) and 80 feet (24 metres) of water at the deepest.

▲ Exploring the wreck or the RMS *Rhone*

The 800-acre park covers not only the area off Salt Island, but Dead Chest Island, as well as a site off Peter Island which contains the anchor that the ship lost as the first blasts of the storm ripped through the harbour. Although the structure of the steel steam ship has corroded with time, much of its skeleton remains intact. The ship's front portion lies on its starboard side and even though its bowsprit is gone, the large copper ring that had held it is still there. A number of portholes remain, as do portions of the hull. Corals cover much of the ship's structure in a palate of colours, and schools of vibrant fish swim in and out of its skeletal remains. The ship has also achieved Hollywood stardom as the backdrop for the underwater scenes in the 1976 film, *The Deep*, starring Jacqueline Bisset and Nick Nolte. All local dive operators and some snorkel tour boats offer trips to the *Rhone*. (For more about the *Rhone*, see 'The Rhone's Last Hours'.)

If you were to be shipwrecked, hope that you're swept up onto Prickly Pear. **Prickly Pear National Park**, a small nature reserve in the middle of North Sound off Virgin Gorda, is fringed with a classic white sand beach. But unlike Robinson Crusoe, you won't have to crack open a coconut to survive since this desert island comes equipped with a beach bar as well beach chairs and some palm-frond shelters. It's bit off the beaten track, so you do need a boat to get here. Some people rent small dinghies in Leverick Bay, which makes the entire North Sound area more accessible.

Located off the southern tip of Virgin Gorda, **Fallen Jerusalem** is a small island primarily comprised of the same style of granite boulders that make up The Baths, and this jumble of rocks obviously inspired its biblical name. It's a unique little island with small pockets of powdery sand interspersed between the rocks. Large waves, though, can make it difficult to anchor a boat here safely in the winter. The island contains a colony of laughing gulls.

West Dog is part of a chain of small rocky islands called 'the Dogs' situated to the north of Virgin Gorda, and is the only one in the uninhabited group that is a national park. The snorkelling is superb and is the main reason to come here, although if you like sea birds, there are plenty in summer. It is a decent day anchorage, although not recommended for overnight.

Dead Chest is a craggy island off the northern tip of Peter Island that is a bird sanctuary. Its coffin-like shape when seen from the sea is the reason for the name, although it is also rumoured that a pirate captain marooned his crew here in days of yore with little more than that proverbial bottle of rum.

The Rhone's last hours

Today the RMS *Rhone*, which lies encrusted in coral off the western point of Salt Island, is the BVI's most popular dive site. Its skeleton, which teems with fish and sea life, is all that is left of one of England's state of the art steam ships tragically sunk by a hurricane in October 1867 with all but 23 of its passengers and crew.

Built by the Millwall Iron Works of England in 1865, the *Rhone* was a sturdily constructed vessel, 310 feet long and weighing 2,738 tons. It had a total of 313 passenger cabins in first, second and third class, and was just two years old when it set out for its fateful voyage to the Caribbean. Her skipper, Captain Wooley, had been heading for the bustling Danish port of St Thomas for coal, water and other supplies, but a yellow fever outbreak on the island forced him to reroute the ship to Peter Island in the British Virgin Islands.

On the morning of 29 October the ship was peacefully at anchor just outside Great Harbour when the barometer began to fall dramatically. At first Wooley was unconcerned. Believing the hurricane season to be over, the skipper felt that the impending storm must be a 'norther'. In fact, the storm was a hurricane that would devastate much of the Virgin Islands. Noting the falling barometer and the rising wind and sea, Captain Wooley and the captain of the *Conway*, a ship also at anchor in the harbour, both realized that action had to be taken. The *Conway* left the harbour first, steaming towards the safety of Road Harbour. The **Rhone**, though, was already in trouble. The anchor chain jammed in the hawse pipe and snapped; the anchor was lost.

In a graphic account written on 3 November 1867, Captain Vesey, who was commissioned by the secretary of the Admiralty, Whitehall, to report on the extent of the hurricane's damage in the islands, described the *Rhone's* last hours. 'The *Rhone's* steam was

▲ An illustration of the RMS *Rhone* from a poster designed by Roger Burnett

up just as the *Conway* left her,' Vesey wrote, 'but Captain Wooley hailed that he could not steam against such a breeze. Shortly after, the *Rhone* began to drag then slipped her cables and endeavoured to sea, but when the drift and rain cleared off, she was next seen on Salt Island. I fear that in the *Rhone* great loss of life occurred. Twenty three only were saved as far as I can yet learn, namely four men who were found on the fore topsail yard, which is above water, a few got on shore and ten others and the fourth officer were found in the Sound clinging to the lifeboat.'

Sailing past Salt Island on the morning of 3 November, Vesey observed the wreck of the RMS Packet *Rhone* first hand: 'Her poop rail was close to a large boulder on the west point, but the hull was standing under water – the foremast was standing, but the vessel herself was broken in two and her head slewed to the north – 50 yards either way – would have put her into a sandy bay.'

Captain Wooley had been swept overboard at the height of the storm, never to be seen again. The graves of some of the crew can still be seen on the western point of Salt Island.

Great Tobago and **Little Tobago** can be found in the westernmost limits of the BVI. Both are bird sanctuaries, and it is lovely to anchor a boat off these islands and watch nesting birds fly in and out. Some of the sea birds commonly seen here include brown boobies, magnificent frigatebirds and tropicbirds, which have a majestic, plume-like tail, and are rarely seen elsewhere in the territory. Frigatebirds are a regionally endangered sea bird and yachtsmen anchoring at Great Tobago are asked not go ashore and disturb them. **Diamond Cay**, off Jost Van Dyke is a rocky, vegetated area that is the smallest of the offshore cays that are parks. It is also a bird sanctuary.

Cam Bay is located on Great Camanoe, a small island just north of Beef Island. **Cam Bay Park** is a nature reserve, and a fine example of a complete coastal ecosystem with all four components – extensive mangroves, seagrass beds, coral reefs and a salt pond on land. The park has a nice little beach and is a good stopover if you want to avoid the normal charter boat circuit. The bay is situated on Great Camanoe's eastern side, within easy reach of Trellis Bay, making it a pleasant day trip. Care should be exercised when visiting this site, since seagrass beds are fragile and are an important food source for turtles.

❾ Keeping active
Things to do on land and sea

ABOVE THE WATER
Term charter boats
For most island visitors, the BVI is about the water. Many spend their entire vacation at sea aboard one of the territory's large selection of charter yachts. For those who like to leave the driving to someone else, there is a handsome collection of fully crewed yachts that come complete with skipper, cook and mate. Others are 'bare' – that is, you, your family and friends are the crew. The BVI was one of the first sailing destinations to promote bareboating in a big way, and it's easy to see why. The close layout of the islands is perfect for tooling around the sea without worry; no anchorage is further than an hour or two from the next, and within the confines of the islands, the roughest the water usually gets is a brisk chop. Whether crewed or bare, the best part of being on a boat is that the entire BVI is at your disposal, from the remotest anchorages to some of the area's most popular bays and beaches.

Day charter boats
Even die-hard landlubbers can easily discover the seduction of sailing by taking a day trip. Sailing aboard one of the BVI's dozen or so day charter boats is an ideal way to experience these special islands and visit places that you would not be able to reach otherwise. Day charter boats, which come in both sailing and powerboat models, usually provide lunch and snorkel gear, and knowledgeable crews offer interesting insights into island history and lore. The typical day sailboat leaves the dock around 9 am and returns between 4 and 5 pm. Some will do half-day and sunset sails as well. Popular destinations include the Norman Island caves, The Baths and Jost Van Dyke, although some boats will suit the itinerary to their guests' whim.

Power boat rentals
From small but serviceable hard-bottomed rubber boats to zippy 30-footers with consoles, an increasing number of power boats are available for rental by the day. Power boats allow you to explore a maximum number of islands and anchorages in just a few hours. Gas is not included in the rental of most power boats.

▲ A charter boat at anchor in Deadman's Bay

Sports fishing and fly fishing

The BVI may not be the best known sports fishing destination, but nonetheless, it has a number of superb fishing grounds and expert sports fishing boats to take you there. The most well known are the North Drop (to the islands' north) and the Seamount (to their south), where world record-size blue and white marlin have been landed

▲ Catch of the day

during the peak billfish season from July to September. Other local game fish include kingfish, dolphin (the fish, not the mammal), wahoo, skipjack, yellowfin and blackfin tuna. Bone fishing in the shallows and flats found throughout the BVI has become an increasingly popular sport in the British Virgin Islands. The fish, which has large silvery scales that act as camouflage in our sparkling waters, is a tenacious fighter and landing one is a challenge.

Other watersports

There are many other ways to get around by sea. Windsurfers, kayaks and surfboards are all available for rent on Tortola and Virgin Gorda, along with lessons for those who want to hone their skills. For the adventurous, there are also firms specializing in parasailing and kiteboarding on both Tortola and Virgin Gorda.

BELOW THE SEA
Scuba diving

This is the ultimate way to explore the BVI's underwater wonders. The many professional dive firms operating in the territory offer a range of services that include day-long introductory courses, often referred to as a 'resort course', and certification courses, which can take several days to a week to complete. Once certified, a diver can rent tanks on his own, though it is highly recommended that visiting divers go with a locally based professional both for safety's sake, and because they know all of the best locales. Rendezvous diving is where a dive boat will meet up with a charter boat, a popular service provided by a number of dive operators.

Snorkelling

The simplest way to explore the area's many beautiful reefs is to go snorkelling. The equipment is simple, requiring just a mask, snorkel and fins, and the technique, even for novices, is easy to master. There are many good snorkelling areas off our beaches, but if you are on a boat, even more of the area's spectacular reefs are within easy reach. Almost all day charter boats have snorkel equipment on board and quite a few of them offer snorkelling instruction. Several boats specialize in snorkelling tours exclusively.

TERRA FIRMA

If lying on a beach soaking up the rays is your idea of the perfect vacation, you've come to the right place. There are dozens of beaches

Skimming down the channel aboard a windsurfer

for this passive sport and no end of beach-towel athletes vying for the gold. But for those who'd like to shake off the sand and sample some of the islands' other activities, there are plenty on offer.

A number of hotels and resorts throughout the islands provide **tennis** courts for their guests. Several, including Nanny Cay, Lambert Beach Resort and Long Bay on Tortola allow non-guests to play for a small fee. The Tortola Sports Club also has several tennis courts and a squash court; a temporary membership is required. Little Dix, Leverick Bay and Biras Creek have tennis courts on Virgin Gorda.

Shadow, whose stable is located at Meyers along the Ridge Road on Tortola, offers **trail rides** to Cane Garden Bay or to Sage Mountain. If you have children and want to give them lessons while you are here, contact Tessa at the Animal Shelter in Road Town.

Biking in the BVI is not for the faint of heart. If you want to ride on level land, the shoreside road that follows the Sir Francis Drake Channel from Road Town to West End is a breathtaking ride. Tortola's Ridge Road, which runs east to west along the island's spine, is another scenic route. Last Stop Sports, located at Port Purcell in Road Town, rents mountain bikes on Tortola, while several resorts on Virgin Gorda, including Little Dix and Biras Creek, offer bikes for their guests. Anegada Reef Hotel on Anegada also rents bikes, a good way to negotiate this flat island, although be careful not to get bogged down in the sand. If you're on Tortola and want to explore the gently rolling hills of the Virgin Gorda Valley, you can always rent a bike in Road Town and take it over on the ferry.

There are no 18-hole **golf** courses in the BVI, but at Captain Mulligan's Driving Range and Leisure Centre on Nanny Cay you can practise your swing by driving floating golf balls into the sea. There is also a miniature golf course at the Mine Shaft on Virgin Gorda.

If you would like to get to know the BVI from the ground up, there is nothing like **walking** through our parks, up our ghuts (rocky waterways) and along our ridges. Two of the most popular walks are at Sage Mountain National Park, where neatly gravelled paths through a variety of tropical environments create a lovely and easy to manage walk. Hiking to the summit of Gorda Peak on Virgin Gorda is another delightful and easy walk. There are also scenic walks through the North Sound resorts of Bitter End and Blras Creek. Shark Bay above Brewer's Bay on its eastern ridge, has several hiking trails that range from easy to difficult. The islands' many ghuts, that lead from the ridges to some of the BVI's less accessible beaches, like Trunk Bay on Tortola's north shore, make for a more challenging hike, but are well worth the effort. On Jost Van Dyke, the road from Great Harbour to White Bay is picturesque and not overly steep. For more leisurely strolls, walk through the Botanic Gardens in Road Town, or the charming village of Carrot Bay on Tortola's north shore.

⑩ An island of delights

Some local fruits and vegetables

Succulent and aromatic, tropical fruits are in a world of their own. Think of a mango, which when fully ripe, literally drips with flavour, or an apricot-coloured papaya, which when icy-cold has the refreshing texture of sherbet. Mangoes, papayas, pineapples, avocados and bananas are the tropical fruits most commonly found in northern supermarkets. But here in the BVI, there are many more, each with its own special appeal. Sugar apples, breadfruit, soursop and guava are among the many tantalising fruits that flourish in these islands.

Some fruit is grown commercially in the BVI although not on a large scale. Some of the supermarkets in Road Town sell local produce, and in the villages you can often find small, family run grocery stores and roadside stands that sell island grown vegetables and fruit, especially mangoes, bananas and papaya, when in season.

▲ A terraced farm plot on Tortola

Many of the fruit and vegetables in the BVI were introduced to the islands by the Amerindians, who brought cassava and other root crops, such as sweet potatoes, here from South America. Additional produce was transported to the West Indies by the Spanish explorers and European traders and planters. Breadfruit, for instance, was brought to the islands from the Pacific by Captain Bligh of *Mutiny on the Bounty* fame, as a staple food for the Caribbean's slave population. As a matter of fact, it is thought that Captain Bligh may have been more concerned about transporting the tree saplings to the New World than he was for his crew, and that this may have contributed to his ship's well-known mutiny.

Once self-sufficient in agriculture and an exporter of produce to nearby islands, the BVI today imports much of its food. Growing vegetables in an inhospitable climate where rainfall is inconsistent, the sun blazingly hot and the insects voracious is a challenge. But along the cooler hillsides, where the soil is more fertile, one can still see small farm plots neatly terraced with local stone. Groves of banana, mangoes and papaya can also be seen on the mountainsides, and occasionally in the valleys and low-lying areas.

BVI farmers have adapted to conditions by growing a large variety of hardy root crops, which are often referred to on local menus as 'provisions'. The sweet potato, like all potatoes, originated in South America. This staple of the European diet was shipped back to the Old World from the New by the Spanish explorers. Dasheen, yams and sweet potatoes are all considered ground provisions. Fruits, like papayas and bananas, that are often boiled while still green are also commonly used as vegetables. A guide to some of the fruits and vegetables commonly grown in the BVI follows.

SUCCULENT FRUITS
Avocado (*Persea americana*)
Some avocados are grown on the islands, although mostly in gardens. The ones in the markets are largely imported. The best fruit comes from grafted trees and it can take eight to 12 years before a tree produces. The fruit originated in Central America and may have been introduced to the Caribbean by the Amerindians. The avocado tree is fairly tall, averaging 30 feet (9 metres), and has pointed dark green leaves. The fruit from different trees varies and can range from green to almost purple in colour; and from pear-like to oval in shape. This fruit, although delicious, is not recommended for dieters: a 1 lb (500 gram) avocado can contain 500 calories.

Bananas and plantains (family Musaceae)

Bananas, which originated some 4,000 years ago in Malaysia, are thought to be the first species of plants domesticated by man. They were brought to Hispaniola by the Spanish and spread from there throughout the West Indies. Most BVI-grown bananas are delicious. The small finger type – or fig banana – are a bit tarter than other varieties, but are meaty, rich and full flavoured. The Gros Michel, Valery and Cavendish are also grown here, but are generally used boiled as a vegetable, rather than eaten as a fruit. The plantain, similar to the banana, but larger, starchier, and less sweet, is generally sliced, fried in oil or butter until golden and served as a side dish.

Breadfruit (*Artocarpus communis*)

This large and dramatic tree can grow to the lofty height of 60 feet (18 metres) and has large, sectioned leaves. You will see it in many BVI gardens, especially those along the islands' ridges. The fruit is large, green and round on the outside, with a ridged skin. The flesh is white and starchy, hence the name, and is often baked in the oven or grilled on top of a coal pot and used as a vegetable.

Coconut (*Cocos nucifera*)

Although coconut palms originated in South East Asia, they are now the emblem of the Caribbean. What tropical beach scene would be complete without them? Coconut palms grow to an impressive 70 feet (21 metres) and they take five to seven years to bear fruit. In the BVI, coconuts are sold commercially on a limited basis, but since most people have a tree in their garden, it's rarely necessary to buy one. They are sometimes used for their water, which when mixed with rum is a popular local drink. When the coconut meat is ground up, mixed with water and strained, coconut milk is produced. Ground or shaved coconut meat is also used in a variety of delicious local cakes and tarts.

Guava (*Psidium guajava*)

This tree, which is native to the Caribbean, has a plum-sized fruit which is yellow green on the outside, and when ripe has sweet pink flesh and a great many seeds on the inside. The tree can grow to 20 feet (6 metres) or more and has small white flowers when in bloom. Local tarts and jam are made from the guava.

Mango (*Mangifera indica*)

British Virgin Islanders love mango season. Syrupy when fully ripe, the fruit can be messy to eat, and on occasion, you will see BV Islanders eating them in the sea – an easy way to enjoy the fruit and wash

▲ Coconuts

up at the same time. The mango grows on a large, shady tree with narrow leaves. The fruit is yellow, although sometimes reddish when ripe, and has a large stone in the centre that makes it tricky to cut open. The best way is to slice it lengthwise down the two wide cheeks along either side of the stone. Cut these in several lengthwise strips, holding the section by the ends. Cut the meat on each section in diagonal strips and flip the strip inside out. The fruit should peel off the skin easily.

Papaya (*Carica papaya*)

Papaya is a fruit that leads a double life. Eaten ripe it's delicious as a breakfast treat, or if cooked when green, it can be used as a nutritious vegetable. Sometimes called 'paw paw', the juice of this versatile fruit is also used as a tenderizer; or it can be blended with yogurt and honey to make a delicious smoothie. The tree itself is ungainly and with its tall, hollow stem, is more like a plant than a tree. The oval-shaped fruit, which turns a lovely yellowy orange colour when ripe, can be as large as a good sized melon.

Passion fruit (*Passiflora edulis*)

Another South American transplant, the passion fruit got its name from the early Spanish missionaries who believed the plant's flower represented the passion of Christ. The flower is spectacular, with a layer of white petals on the outside and a frilly fringe on the inside. In the BVI, the most commonly found fruit is yellow, although it can also be a deep purple. Inside, the fruit is filled with small brown pips,

▲ Papayas

which can be removed by soaking in water and then straining. It makes a delicious drink.

Pineapple (*Ananas comosus*)

Most people think of Hawaii when they think of pineapple, but the fruit is actually native to the West Indies and Central America. And even though it's not as prolific here as elsewhere, our BVI grown pineapples are small and sweet. The plant can be grown by cutting off its prickly crown, and planting it into the ground. The pineapple takes about ten months to grow.

Sour sop (*Annona muricata*)

This prickly looking fruit is oval, almost heart shaped, and has a dimpled green skin. Don't let its homely looks fool you. Inside the sour sop has a creamy white flesh that is at its best when blended into ice cream, sherbets and drinks. The fast growing tree has small shiny leaves and yellowy green flowers.

Sugar apple (*Annona Squamosa*)

This fruit is also known as the custard apple and it is one of the BVI's sweetest confections. The sticky fruit has white flesh which, as its

▲ Sugar apples

name implies, is the consistency of custard. Heart-shaped and about the size of a tennis ball, the fruit is green and segmented on the outside and filled with lots of seeds on the inside.

PROVISIONS, PUMPKINS AND OTHER GOURDS
Cassava (*Manihot esculenta*)
This shrub was brought to the islands by the Amerindians, who dried its root, ground it into a fine flour and then formed it into a flat bread which they baked on a pottery griddle. A poison called prussic acid is found in the cassava, which must be removed by cooking or pressing. Cassava bread cooked on an iron griddle can still be found in local markets. The root, which has a slightly stringy texture when boiled, is also eaten as a vegetable.

Christophene (*Sechium edule*)
This unusual gourd has a firm white flesh and originally came to the islands via Mexico. It is oval in shape and it can have dimpled skin that is a pale green. If you eat at a local restaurant, christophene is often served as a side dish. Cooked correctly, it should be slightly crisp in texture; overcooked it can become mushy.

Dasheen (*Colocasia esculenta*)
Dasheen is among the popular root crops grown in the BVI. Like most tubers here, it is boiled and eaten as a side dish. The plant itself is about 4 or 5 feet high (1.5 metres) and has large leaves. The leaves, which are spinach-like in size and texture, are sometimes used in a soup called callaloo.

Peppers (*Capsicum* spp.)
Peppers are grown throughout the BVI, but they are generally of the hot variety. They are often used to make hot sauce, which is liberally sprinkled onto all sorts of food from peas and rice to stewed chicken. These sauces, which are made with onions, spices and vinegar, can be found in the supermarket, but beware: they can be fiery. Scotch bonnets and the smaller bird peppers, which come in a lovely range of green, yellow and red, are the peppers commonly grown here.

Pumpkin (*Cucurbita* spp.)
The West Indian pumpkin is different from the bright orange variety found in North America, especially at Halloween. In the BVI this popular gourd is mottled green and yellow. Its rind is tougher and there is more meat inside, but like its North American counterparts it can grow impressively big. Its origins are uncertain and it has been cultivated for so long that its wild form no longer exists. Here in the

▲ A medley of local vegetables and fruit

BVI the meat is cooked as a vegetable; or simmered and pureed with a meat broth and cream, it is a popular soup. The pumpkin grows on vines that trail along the ground and have a large, creamy coloured flower. For an unusual treat, dip the flower in batter and deep fry.

Sugar cane (*Saccharum officinarum*)

Sugar was once the mainstay of the BVI economy, and one of its largest exports. But following the end of slavery in 1834 and the eventual collapse of the plantation economy, it was grown primarily for home consumption and to supply the few remaining rum distilleries. Very little sugar cane is grown in the BVI today, but when you drive through the countryside, you will still see some stands of this tall member of the grass family. Its flowers are like feathery plumes and the sugar is extracted by crushing the large stalks. Children will often peel the stalk and suck on the sweet meat inside like a large peppermint stick.

Sweet potato (*Ipomoea batatas*)

The sweet potato is native to the New World and was cultivated by the Aztecs before being taken to Europe by the Spaniards in the sixteenth century. Today it is the tropics' most important root crop and, here in the BVI, this starchy and just slightly sweet tuber is a popular side dish.

Talking about sweet potatoes can be confusing since they are often referred to as yams (see 'Yam' below), although the true yam comes from a different plant altogether. Adding to the confusion is the fact that the 'Louisiana yam', a bright orange tuber that is often served in America at Thanksgiving, is actually a sweet potato. It originated from a variety of sweet potato found in Puerto Rico and got its name from American slaves who called it 'yam' because the root reminded them of a starchy, edible tuber called 'nyami' that grew in their Senegalese homeland.

Like the white potato, the sweet potato can be boiled, mashed with butter or baked. Rich in vitamin C and carbohydrates, it is very good for you.

Yam (*Dioscorea* sp.)

The yam is occasionally confused with the sweet potato, but they are actually from different families (the sweet potato is part of the morning glory family). Yams can grow very large, sometimes weighing as much as an impressive 20 lb (9 kg). The interior is dense white and sometimes contains reddish fibre. Like all local root crops, yams are a popular side dish.

⑪ Buds, bushes and trees

Bright and colourful, flowers embellish the BVI, and brighten our tropical days. They can be found tamed in gardens and strewn wild throughout the territory's verges and hillsides. Most of the BVI's brightest blooms are transplants from other parts of the world – East Asia, the South Pacific and South and Central America. Our native flowers are less splashy, being pastel-hued and subtly formed. They can be found in the most unlikely places, on a vine scrambling up a telephone pole, or adorning a scraggly little plant growing on the side of the road. Native or newcomer, flowers are an integral part of our tropical environment. The J. R. O'Neal Botanic Gardens in Road Town, which contains a rich array of exotic and indigenous plants, is an ideal place to learn more about our BVI flowers. As you walk through the gardens or drive around the islands, keep an eye out for some of these common tropical flowers.

THE NEWCOMERS
Allamanda (*Allamanda cathartica*)
With its profusion of bright yellow flowers, the allamanda has a sunny disposition that is a welcoming presence in many BVI gardens. The flowers have a trumpet-like form and are between 4 and 6 inches (10 and 15 cm) wide. Some varieties of this cheerful Brazilian native like to climb and can be seen gracing arbours and fences. The pointed leaves are deep green and shiny.

Bougainvillea (*Bougainvillea* spp.)
Bougainvillea is a fascinating plant. It has paper-lantern shaped bracts in bright colours like magenta, purple and orange, that are often mistaken for flowers. The actual flower though, is small, delicate and white, and sits inconspicuously inside the bract. The bush blooms often, especially in drier conditions, making it popular in BVI gardens, where rain can be sporadic. Originally from Brazil, the bougainvillea is a climbing plant and can often be seen scaling fences and trees. Sharp thorns on its stems help it to climb, but make it painful to trim.

Hibiscus (*Hibiscus* spp.)
Almost every BVI garden has at least one, if not several, hibiscus bushes. This bush comes in a startling range of colours and varieties. There are about 200 species of hibiscus, and because this is a popular plant to hybridize, there may be more on the way. The hibiscus is from the mallow family of plants that also includes okra and the hollyhock.

▲ The hibiscus comes in a dazzling range of colours

Colours of this originally Asian plant include bright reds, several shades of pink, orange, yellow and even a non-tropical looking grey.

Ixora *(Ixora macrothyrsa, Ixora coccinea)*

This is an import from the East Indies. It comes in red, which is the most common colour, as well as white and pink, and has clusters of tiny flowers grouped to form a grapefruit-sized ball. The leaves are dark green and very shiny.

Oleander *(Nerium oleander)*

Oleander is a hardy plant with a delicate flower and a powerful defence system, making it one of the BVI's most prevalent garden plants. Roaming livestock can play havoc with BVI gardens, but the oleander's poisonous sap keeps them at bay, and it is often used as a hedge. Originally an import from the Mediterranean and Asia, it can grow up to 25 feet (7.5 metres) tall, although most people keep it neatly trimmed.

◀ A window frames a vibrant bougainvillea

THE NATIVES
Orchids

There are more than 20,000 species of orchid, many of which are now hybridized. The Botanic Gardens has an orchid pavilion with several species on display, but they also grow wild. The local varieties are small and delicate with yellow or pink flowers that grow atop a willowy stalk. This unusual plant should be admired but not disturbed.

The century plant (*Agave Americana*)

In the spring, the BVI's hillsides are dotted with the impressive flowers of the century plant, a gigantic succulent whose leaves grow 6 feet

▲ A century plant in bloom

(2 metres) long. Every seven or so years, the plant puts out a lanky stalk which ranges from 15 to 30 feet (4.5 to 9 metres) and is festooned with chrome yellow flowers. The stalk and the flower pods eventually dry to a dull brown. Just before the holidays, the stalk is cut down, the flowers pods are sprayed gold and silver and the plant is reincarnated as a BVI-style Christmas tree.

Other wild flowers include the **soldier's tassel** (*Emilia sonchifolia*). Also known as the cupid's paintbrush, this inconspicuous plant produces diminutive reddish-pink flowers shaped like a brush and tipped with gold. The **butterfly weed** (*Asclepias curassavica*), sometimes called the blood flower, is also small and retiring, but has bright red petals and a yellow stamen.

FLOWERING TREES

Two of the most showy trees in the BVI are the frangipani and the flamboyant. A highly fragrant tree, the **frangipani** (*Plumeria rubra, Plumeria acutifolia*) has pink, yellow or white flowers. Its stalks, which

▲ Creamy white frangipani blossoms

grow to around 15 feet (4.5 metres) are like that of a succulent and its sap is caustic. A smaller, wild variety with narrow, pointed leaves and white flowers grows throughout the islands' hillsides, often clinging precariously to a rocky hillside. The flower of the **flamboyant** (*Delonix regia*), also known as the poinciana, is scarlet red and when the tree is in full bloom in local gardens, it is a spectacular sight. The tree originated in Madagascar, but is now ubiquitous throughout the Caribbean.

The **white cedar** (*Tabebuia heterophylla*) is the British Virgin Islands' national tree. A tropical American tree related to the mahogany family, it is inconspicuous until it bursts into pink or white flowers throughout the islands. The white cedar is indigenous to the British Virgin Islands and is not related to the cedar common to northern climates (*Arborvitae*). The **ficus** (*Ficus benghalensis*) is one of the Islands' largest trees, growing to an impressive 80 feet (24 metres) in height and forming a vast umbrella of shade. It has aerial roots that attach themselves to the ground, forming secondary trunks. The ficus is of the Moraceae or mulberry family which includes the India-rubber tree and a fruit-bearing fig common in the Mediterranean. The **mahogany** is the common name for a member of the Meliaceae family. Mahogany trees once covered the mountainsides of the British Virgin Islands, but were logged heavily during the plantation era; and while some were used locally, most were exported to Europe. Many of the mahoganies seen on Tortola, including many of those at Sage Mountain National Park, have been replanted.

The **seagrape** (*Cocoloba uvifera*) along with the coconut tree, is the most commonly seen plant growing along our shorelines. It has large, almost round, rubbery leaves and grows best in sandy soil. Its pods of fruit grow in grape-like clusters and are used to make a local jam. **Manchioneel** (*Hippomane manicinella*) is one tree that it is best to avoid in a rain shower. This tree, which grows along less-frequented beaches, especially on the outer islands, is highly poisonous. Both its fruit and its leaves, which produce a milky sap, should be avoided since they can cause severe blistering. The leaves of the tree are 2 to 4 inches long (5 to 10 cm) and grow on long stalks.

One of the BVI's unique trees is the **mangrove**, which has the unusual ability to thrive in warm, salty environments. Like a biological desalination plant, the mangrove's long extended roots take up salt water and transform it into fresh. There are three types of mangroves

◀ A scarlet flamboyant

▲ Mangroves thrive in a salty environment

in the BVI: red (*Rizophora mangle*), black (*Avicennia germinans*) and white (*Languncularia racemosa*). Mangroves grow along the shoreline where their dense root system acts as a nursery for young sea life and filters out silt coming off the land, keeping our water clean and protecting the area's coral reefs. In turn, they also protect the shore from high waves and erosion.

BUSH REMEDIES

The BVI's prodigious plantlife provides a lush and colourful backdrop for island homes that is easy to take for granted. But for generations, many of our most common plants had a much more important function. From easing the symptoms of the common cold to relieving toothache, plants were many islanders' only source of medicine.

Bush medicine has its roots in Amerindian culture, where the shaman would use spells and potent herbs to cure the sick. Much of today's knowledge of bush medicine though, was brought here from Africa and Europe during the early plantation era. Today, knowledge of bush medicine has grown with the migration of people from other parts of the Caribbean to the British Virgin Islands; and even with modern medicines readily available, islanders will often brew up a soothing batch of bush tea to sooth the nerves or relieve a bout of rheumatism.

▲ A painkiller tree in the J. R. O'Neal Botanic Gardens

One of the most common plants found outside British Virgin Islands homes is **lemon grass** (*Cymbopogon citratus*). This grass is rich in a substance called citral, the active ingredient in lemon peel, which is said to aid in digestion as well as relieve spasms, muscle cramps, rheumatism and headaches. Lemon grass is most commonly brewed into a gentle and pleasant tasting tea, but is also used as a flavouring in food.

The **guava** tree (*Psidium guajava L*) is best known for its sweet fruit used in rum punch and local jam, but its leaves and buds can also be made into a tea to cure dysentery and parasites.

Other traditionally used medicinal plants include the **love leaf** (*Kalanchoe pinata*), also known as the tree of life, whose leaves are brewed into a tea to relieve urinary problems, hypertension and stomach ailments. The aptly named **worry wine** (*Stachytarpheta jamaicensis*) is drunk as a tea and used for high blood pressure and diabetes. The **inflammation bush** (*Verbesine alata*) is brewed into a tea that has traditionally been used by women after giving birth or to relieve menstrual cramps. The **periwinkle** (*Vinca rosea*) is a bright and cheerful plant with pink and mauve flowers which also has a practical side. Its leaves, brewed into a tea, have been used to treat diabetes.

Cotton (*Gossipium barbadense*) was grown here by the Amerindians and later raised for export by the early planters. Tea made from its leaves though, has also been used for relieving fevers. A tea made from the **mimosa** (*Mimosa pudica*) known as the 'sensitive plant' because its leaves close when touched, has been used to calm whooping cough. The leaves of the tropical **painkiller tree** (*Morinda citrifolia*) are used as poultices for wounds and to relieve pain in joints. The fruit is called *noni* and its juice, which is high in vitamin C, is used to treat colds and influenza, among other illnesses.

Perhaps the best known of local medicinal plants is the **aloe** (*Aloe vera*). The jelly filled centre of this succulent plant is extremely effective for soothing sunburned skin and healing other types of burns. In other parts of the world it is commercially added to cosmetics and skin lotions. The **bush bath** is a fragrant Virgin Islands tradition. Made from the leaves of almost a dozen plants, it can include Christmas bush, balsam, black sage, ginger, lemon grass and sweet scent. Most bush bath devotees take it for no other reason than that it feels good. Another bath is made from the root of the **congo** or 'strong man' plant (*Pettiveria alliacea*).

Many of these medicinal plants, as well as others, can be found in the J. R. O'Neal Botanic Gardens' Bush and Herb Garden in Road Town.

Even though there is a growing movement in western cultures to use traditional remedies, common sense must always prevail; the use of any herbal medicine should not be a substitute for proper medical treatment.

⑫ Going wild

Animals and birds of the BVI

Some of the creatures in the British Virgin Islands are endemic, others have been introduced, but whether it's a bird, frog or lizard, all of the BVI's unique creatures add to the richness of its environment. Chirping frogs that sound like birds, birds with gigantic wing spans and lizards that perform death-defying leaps are just a few of the entertaining species that you will encounter as you wander through our parks, beaches and rural areas. You'll also be happy to note that none of our creatures, including our minute and rarely seen scorpions, pack a punch much worse than a bee sting.

▲ The gecko is a commonly seen Virgin Islands lizard

LIZARDS

These fascinating reptiles abound in the BVI. You will see them rustling through the leaves of our gardens and catching moths on the side of our walls. Adaptable creatures, they live as happily indoors, where they perform the valuable service of eating mosquitoes and other pesky insects, as they do outside. Agile as an acrobat, it's not uncommon to see a lizard leap from the top of a high wall, shake its small head and then scoop an insect up from the ground. We have 11 types of lizards in the BVI, the most common of which are the anoles. The **crested anole**, locally called the man lizard, has a spiked crown and is often observed puffing up his voluminous yellow, green and red throat fan to defend his territory or woo a lady. The female is smaller and has a yellow stripe down her back. The **southern woodslave** is a member of the gecko family and is often seen darting up walls to catch an unsuspecting moth. His amazing wall-climbing ability is created by tiny flaps of skin on his flattened toes called lamellae, each of which carries hundreds of tiny hooks that catch onto even the smoothest surface. The **Virgin Gorda gecko**, which measures a mere half to three-quarters of an inch (12 to 20 mm), is endemic to the BVI and is the world's smallest lizard. At the other end of the scale, the **ground lizard** is a large (generally 8 inches, 20 cm long) and ungainly creature that lumbers through the undergrowth in a snake-like fashion, its legs stretched outwards and its long body hugging the ground. The **slipperyback lizard**, also known as the skink, is endangered in the BVI and threatened in the rest of the world. Metallic bronze in colour, it is 6 inches (15 cm) long and is the only local species that gives birth to live young.

IGUANAS

The **Anegada iguana** (*Cyclura pinguis*) is an impressive 5-foot (1.5-metre) long creature that was once prevalent throughout Puerto Rico and the Virgin Islands, but is now found only in the BVI. Its primary home is Anegada, although they are also found on Guana and Necker Islands. The iguana is heavy set with large chunky legs, is a dark steely grey and has a low, zigzag-shaped crest running down the centre of his back. He is a reclusive fellow that prefers to live in the bushy areas in Anegada's interior, and is not easily spotted. Because of disappearing habitat and predation by wild cats, the reptile is endangered. In an effort to save the species, the National Parks Trust raises juvenile iguanas in a facility called Headstart located in Anegada's Settlement. Once they are too large to become a tasty meal for a predator, they are released into the wild.

▲ The Anegada iguana *(copyright John Binns, by courtesy of the National Parks Trust)*

A native of Mexico and South America, the **green iguana** (*Iguana iguana*) is also found here in the BVI. These reptiles can grow as large as 4 feet (1.2 metres) and are primarily found in the Virgin Gorda North Sound area and on Peter Island, where they can be seen crossing the road or lounging on a rock.

OTHER INTERESTING CREATURES
Whistling frogs (genus *Eleutherodactylus*)
There are three native whistling frogs in the BVI. The one that gets the most attention is the 'bo peep' frog, as it is called locally, which has a loud chirping call that sounds more like that of a cricket or bird than the croak of a frog. Small, just 2 or 3 inches (5 to 7 cm) long, and pale beige in colour, it likes to hide in flower pots and dense foliage and bursts into robust song whenever there is a rain shower. It is from the same family of whistling frogs known as the coqui, which are prevalent in Puerto Rico.

The red-footed tortoise (*Geochelone carbonaria*)
Like the Anegada iguana, these creatures were once a common sight here. Today, only a few can be found, including several at the Botanic Gardens and at Little Secrets Nature Gallery on Virgin Gorda. A number have been reintroduced to the wild on Guana Island. The tortoise is a distinctive looking fellow with red spots on its feet and orange colouring around its mouth.

The mongoose (*genus Herpestes*)
The mongoose is a cunning and lightning-fast creature that is most commonly spotted darting across the road at breakneck speed.

▲ A whistling tree frog

Closely related to the civet and the larger ichneumon of Africa, the mongoose is a small carnivorous mammal about the size of a mink and the shape of a weasel. Originally from India, they were introduced here by the planters to protect the cane fields from a burgeoning population of rats. Now it's considered a nuisance, since it also devours eggs, poultry and other small creatures.

OUR BIRDS

From song birds to sea birds, there are 160 species of birds present in the BVI. Like our winter vacationers, some of the islands' land and sea birds are migratory, flying in for a warm weather vacation from up north. Others are homebodies, making the islands a year-round abode. Perhaps 90 per cent of the birds that inhabit the BVI are also found in North America, and just a handful or so are native solely to the Caribbean. A few of the most commonly seen birds follow.

The land birds

The legend goes that Columbus named the BVI's largest island 'Tortola' (the Spanish word for dove) because he saw such an abundance of these birds as he sailed by in 1493. The **zenaida** (*Zenaida aurita*) is one of the most common of the islands' doves. About 10 to 11 inches (25 cm) long with a round tail and a white band on its wing tips, the

The zenaida was once found in the BVI in abundance

zenaida can also be recognized by its cooing sound, which is similar to that of a mourning dove. Locally it is called the mountain dove. As its name implies, the **ground dove** (*Columbina passerina*) spends a lot of time hopping along unpaved roads as it feeds, flying close to the ground in short bursts. It is about 6 to 7 inches (16 cm) long and has purple-grey feathers. It nests in low bushes or trees or directly on the ground.

The **American kestrel** (*Falco sparverius*), locally called the 'killy killy', can be seen soaring effortlessly astride the many updrafts and air currents prevalent in the BVI's steep valleys. This is a small falcon, around 9 to 12 inches (24 to 30 cm), but has the species' signature hooked beak and is distinguished by its mottled facial pattern and its red tail, which has a broad black terminal band. You may also see it sitting atop telephone poles, where it can easily spot a lizard or snake for dinner. The **green-throated carib** (*Sericotes holosericeus*) is a delight to watch. Sometimes called the doctor bird, it can often be seen darting at lightning speed in and out of flowering shrubs. The iridescent green hummingbird has a sapphire blue mark on the breast. At 4 to 5 inches (10 to 12 cm), it is considered large for the species. Another dainty and beautifully coloured bird found here in the BVI is the yellow-breasted **bananaquit** (*Coereba flaveola*). Only about 4 to 5 inches (10 to 12 cm) tall, the bird can often be seen sipping on the nectar of the islands' tropical flowers. In order to attract the bird, many residents hang a bird feeder filled with sugar water in their gardens. The **gray kingbird** (*Tyrannus dominicensis*) is more subtly attired than the bananaquit, but makes up for its plain colouring with its melodic chirping. About 9 inches (22 cm) long, grey on top and pale grey-white on the abdomen and breast, it has a distinct black mark extending under the eye to the ear. On the top of its head is a yellow and orange mark. Locally the bird is called the chichery and is often seen perched on telephone wires.

▲ A green-throated carib hummingbird tends its nest

Sea birds and wading birds

With its 7-foot (2.1-metre) wing span, gracefully arched wings and double forked tail, the **magnificent frigatebird** (*Fregata magnificens*) is one of the BVI's most dramatic-looking birds and one of its most accomplished flyers. They can spend days in the air and often sleep in-flight. The male frigatebird is all black with glossy green and purple feathers on the back and a red throat-pouch which it inflates like a balloon to attract females during the mating season. The female is black with a white breast. One of the most familiar sea birds is the **brown pelican** (*Pelecanus occidentalis*), which is often seen swooping into the sea from lofty heights in order to scoop up

▲ Brown pelicans alight on a dinghy

a large bill-full of fish. Clumsy on land, this large bird (averaging 42 to 54 inches, 106 to 137 cm) is more graceful in the air. Unlike other sea birds, the pelican's neck is drawn back onto the shoulders and is not extended in flight. If you are powerboating through the BVI, you may find that the **brown booby** (*Sula leucogaster*) is a travelling companion. This distinctive bird with its sleek brown head and upper body is about 28 inches (70 cm) long and can sometimes be seen hitching a ride on air currents. It nests on the ground. The **royal tern** (*Sterna maxima*) is most often seen in the summer when it comes to shore to breed and least commonly seen in the winter when it spends its time at sea. White to mottled white, the tern has dark wing tips and an entirely black head in summer, while in the winter its forehead is white. The royal tern ranges from 18 to 21 inches (46 to 53 cm) in length. The **laughing gull** (*Laurus atricilla*) is a common sight in the BVI and is easily recognized by its raucous, laughter-like cry. During the breeding season, the laughing gull is distinguished from other West Indian gulls and terns by its black head; at other times it is mottled. The body is light and the wings dark.

▲ A flock of laughing gulls

The **great blue heron**, standing majestically along the shore, makes an impressive sight. At 42 to 52 inches (106 to 132 cm) in length, this is the largest heron in the BVI. It is blue-grey in colour and is often seen wading in shallow mangrove areas. It is rarely seen in the summer, when it breeds in remote areas. Other common BVI wading birds include the smaller **little blue heron** (*Florida caerulea*), which is generally 22 to 28 inches (55 to 71 cm) long and the stately **great egret** (*Egretta alba*), which has a yellow bill and long black legs and stands about 36 to 41 inches (92 to 103 cm) tall. The **cattle egret** (*Bubulcus ibis*) is smaller (21 to 25 inches, 53 to 63 cm). This ominpresent bird actually spends little time near the water; instead it can be seen in the islands' many cattle pastures, often sitting on the back of a contented cow as it feeds off insects. Appropriately, British Virgin Islanders call it 'the tick bird'. The cattle egret ranges from 19 to 25 inches (48 to 63 cm) in size and has a thick, yellowish bill.

▲ The great egret stands by the shore

The flamingos return

Tall, elegant and the colour of a Caribbean sunset, the roseate flamingo is one of Anegada's most magnificent sights. Thousands of this striking bird once populated the salt ponds of Anegada, but by 1950 they had all but disappeared, the victim of hunters who plundered the flocks for their meat and for the feathers used on fashionable ladies' hats.

In 1992 though, in a project coordinated by the British Virgin Islands National Parks Trust, the bird was reintroduced to the island. Working with the National Parks Trust were specialists from the Bermuda Aquarium, who supplied 20 roseate flamingos, and the Conservation Agency from Rhode Island, who oversaw their release.

Flamingos are highly social creatures and even 20 birds is short of the minimum breeding stock, which is generally in the hundreds. But it was a good start. For the next two years, members of the National Parks Trust and the Conservation Agency waited for the flamingos to acclimatize to their new environment, and although the birds exhibited appropriate courtship behaviour and began to build nests, nothing happened until four wild flamingos unexpectedly joined the flock. Within the year, five flamingo chicks hatched and the population has continued to grow each year. Although the birds are yet to number in the thousands, there are 50 birds on Anegada, with another transplanted population doing well on a private nature reserve on Guana Island.

▲ A trio of roseate flamingos

The primary diet of this wading bird is the brine shrimp and other minute aquatic creatures containing carotene, which are abundant in the salt ponds of Anegada and Guana where the birds congregate. It is the carotene that gives the flamingo its rosy hue.

The roseate, which is one of seven species of flamingo world-wide, feeds by straining water through special filtering plates along the inside of its bill that trap its food. It is the largest of the world's species and can reach 5 feet (1.5 metres) in height. The nests are constructed of mud and usually only one egg is laid at a time which both parents incubate. Fluffy and white when born, the chicks are like the proverbial ugly duckling, retaining a light grey colouration until they turn that dramatic pink hue later in maturity.

Flamingos are shy. When visiting the island of Anegada, keep a sharp eye out for them. You are likely to see them standing on the edge of the island's several large salt ponds, but probably from a great distance. Statuesque and graceful, these wonderful birds like their privacy.

⓭ Our underwater kingdom

CREATURES OF THE SEA

The underwater world of the British Virgin Islands is as beautiful as that above water, but with many more surprises. If you are a scuba diver, virtually all of the BVI's marine treasures are at your disposal, but even if you're not, a snorkel and mask will unlock the door to much of this colourful kingdom.

The coral reef is a vast underwater community sheltering an astounding array of creatures. Slinky moray eels, rainbow coloured parrot fish, pastel hued sponges and vermilion starfish live side by side in this well-balanced ecosystem that is essential to the health of our marine world. The builder of the coral reef is the polyp, an inconspicuous creature that does some mighty things. Closely related to the sea anemone, the tiny, tube-shaped polyp anchors itself to rocks or sunken ships and catches minute plankton that float by with its fringe of tentacles. If it is a hard coral, it secretes an outer skeleton of calcium carbonate shaped like a limestone cup.

▼ A diver explores a coral reef inhabited by a school of French grunts

▲ A queen angel fish

For the most part, corals develop polyp by polyp, growing in size and complexity. Branching and multiplying into flower-like structures, the coral grows upwards towards the sun. As time goes on, physical and chemical reactions consolidate these elements into solid coralline limestone. These are your elegant elkhorn and staghorn corals, among others. The **elkhorn**, which has flattened palmate branches, can be found in virtual forests on the sea floor that cover several acres. Colonies can grow 6 to 10 feet (2 to 3 metres) tall. The **staghorn** has 1-inch (2.5 cm) thick branches and can reach 7 feet (2.1 metres) in height. In the dense, rock-shaped **brain coral**, the polyps remain close together until they become united into a compact, cranium-shaped unit. Not all corals are hard to the touch. **Sea whips**, **sea plumes** and **sea fans** have flexible horny skeletons and only small amounts of carbonate. These graceful corals dance to the movements of the sea and its currents. Most corals are benign, although snorkellers should beware of **fire coral**. This aptly named coral contains tiny pores through which minuscule stinging tentacles project.

Corals reproduce in a fascinating once-a-year display that has become a local diving attraction. No one knows exactly how or why they do this, but each year in August, corals spawn simultaneously, releasing millions of eggs into the sea, creating an ethereal milky film. These eggs develop into small larvae which will eventually settle on a rock or other surface and develop into a polyp, thus continuing the process of reef building.

Within these reefs live a fabulous array of creatures from the comical to the grotesque; from the flamboyantly beautiful to organisms that are so well camouflaged, you would swear they were never there. One of the most common and beautifully coloured of these reef fish is the **stoplight parrot fish**. These fish, which come in a stunning variety of colours including red, turquoise and aqua, are more than just a pretty face. By ingesting coral and excreting the smallest of particles, they contribute to the production of sand for our lovely white beaches. The **queen angelfish** (*Holacanthus ciliaris*) is aptly named. This beauty grows to between 8 and 15 inches (20 and 38 cm) long and has striking blue and yellow colouring. The **squirrelfish** (*Holocentrus rufus*) is about a foot (30 cm) long and has distinctive mottled red colouring, edged in a filmy blue. Only 2 to 3 inches (50 to 75 mm) long, the **blue chromis** (*Chromis cyanea*) makes up for its small size with its vivid blue colouring. It is most often found in deeper offshore reefs. The **wrasses** (*Labridae*) form one of the largest tropical fish families. Most are small, between 3 and 6 inches (7.5 and 15 cm) on average, although the **Spanish hogfish** can grow to 15 inches (38 cm). They come in a range of iridescent colours including blue, yellow, silver and mauve. The **trumpetfish** (*Aulostomus maculatus*) is an unusual looking

▼ A trumpetfish

fellow. Long and thin, he sometimes swims upright, looking more like a saxophone than a trumpet. He can grow to between 18 and 30 inches (45 and 76 cm) in length. The **rock hind** (*Epinephelus adscensionis*), like most groupers, is not the reef's most dazzling character, but he is among its most common. Around 8 to 15 inches long (20 to 38 cm), this ungainly fish has reddish brown spots and a pug face that only a mother could love.

A FEW CREATURES TO AVOID

Most of our sea creatures are benign, but here are a few of the ones you should avoid. The **long-spined sea urchin** (*Diadema antillarum*) is one reef dweller that you should look out for. The spikes of these spiny black balls can grow up to 16 inches (40 cm) long and break off when touched, embedding themselves in the skin causing pain and swelling. If this happens to you, try to remove as many of the spines as possible and apply antiseptic or ammonia. The **spotted scorpionfish** (*Scorpaena plumieri*) is one of our best-kept secrets. This master of camouflage, with his stubby body and homely face, looks very much like a coral-encrusted rock. But don't be fooled, he's not as benign as he looks; this rock moves and, if touched, can cause a painful sting. The **moon jellyfish** (*Aurelia aurita*) and the **stinging jellyfish** (*Dactylometra quinquecirrha*) are two more underwater organisms that are best avoided. When brushed, they can cause irritation and a rash.

WHERE TO SNORKEL ...

Exploring the BVI's spectacular underwater world is amazingly easy, even for those without a boat, since many of the territory's coral reefs lie off our beaches and shores. On Tortola, Smuggler's Cove has a reef right off the beach, and although storms have taken their toll on the coral close in, if you snorkel to its outer fringes there is still plenty to see. Brewer's Bay and Cane Garden Bay also have reefs within swimming distance of the beach, and on Long Bay Beef Island you can snorkel the grassy area on its western end. There is plenty of fish life to be seen darting playfully amongst the rocks that line the water's edge at The Baths and Devil's Bay on Virgin Gorda. White Bay on Jost Van Dyke offers another good snorkelling site and it's an easy swim from the beach. The reef off Loblolly Bay on Anegada is one of the area's most dramatic close to shore reefs, but be careful in the winter when the northerly swells are up.

◀ A snorkeller enjoys watching a school of sergeant majors

If you are on a boat, there is excellent snorkelling at the Indians, a series of tall, jagged rocks off Norman Island that some imaginative mariner thought looked like an Indian headdress. The Indians' steep walls are a dramatic backdrop for a colourful array of underwater life. There can be a strong current here, so make sure you are an accomplished snorkeller before trying this area. The caves at Norman Island are easier snorkelling and almost as rewarding. Parrot fish, squirrelfish and wrasse abound along the area's rocky shoreline. The reefs at the Dogs, a group of uninhabited islands to the west of Virgin Gorda, are in good condition and are home to a wide range of corals and fishes.

...AND SCUBA DIVE

Scuba diving opens a whole new perspective on the BVI's marine realm. If you are a certified diver, and go with one of the territory's dozen or so professional dive operators, most of the BVI's spectacular underwater sites will be yours to explore. For beginner or novice divers, these same firms will offer a 'Discover Scuba Diving' course. This introductory lesson, which is sometimes referred to as a 'resort course', usually starts off with a classroom lesson and an initial dive in a pool or shallow beach area to get the student acquainted with the equipment. Then it's off to one of the area's easily accessible offshore reefs for an unforgettable first-time experience. The whole procedure takes half a day.

One of the BVI's most popular dive spots is **Blonde Rock**, which lies between Dead Chest and Salt Island. This pinnacle goes from a depth of 15 feet (4.5 metres) at its shallowest to 60 feet (18 metres) at its deepest. There is plenty to explore here including rock ledges, tunnels, caves and overhangs which are home to a myriad of marine life. **Painted Walls** is a shallow-water dive that ranges from 20 feet to 30 feet (6 to 9 metres) in depth. Four long gullies are lined with corals and sponges. It is found off the southern point of Dead Chest. **Santa Monica Rock** is a bit further out (about a mile south of Norman Island) and since it goes from 10 to 100 feet (3 to 30 metres) is a more challenging dive. Spotted eagle rays, tarpon and other pelagic fish can be seen here. **Alice in Wonderland** is also a good dive for the experienced diver. This underwater wall located at South Bay on Ginger Island slopes down to 100 feet (30 metres). Giant mushroom-shaped corals give the site its name. **Great Dog** and **Seal Dog** are both fine diving areas, although Great Dog is better for beginners. There are spectacular rock formations, canyons and ledges at Seal Dog, but the area is best left to those with experience.

▲ The shipwreck of the *Beata*

There are a number of shipwrecks to explore in the BVI, the most famous of which is the **Rhone** (see Chapter 8), a royal mail ship which went down during a hurricane in 1867. The ship lies in 20 to 80 feet (6 to 24 metres) of water off the western point of Salt Island. The Rhone's anchor found off Peter Island is another popular dive site. Others shipwrecks include the **Marie L**, the **Pat** and the **Beata**, which lie at a site near Cooper Island's Manchioneel Bay known locally as 'Wreck Alley'. The area is marked by a National Parks Trust mooring. A third wreck, the **Barge and Grill**, is located a little to the north of the other wrecks. The **Chikuzen** is a 246-foot (74-metres) refrigerator boat which sank 6 miles (10 km) north of Beef Island in 1981. It is teeming with fish of every description.

Taking good care of our reefs is of utmost importance, and one of the biggest dangers to these fragile ecosystems are boat anchors.

Because of this, the National Parks Trust (NPT) requires the use of their moorings when visiting the following areas: The Baths, Pelican Island, Carrot Shoal, Peter, Norman, Ginger and Cooper Islands; the wreck of the *Fearless*, Dead Chest, Blonde Rock, the Dogs, Guana Island, the *Rhone* and *Rhone's* anchor. All users of the moorings must have a valid NPT moorings permit which can be obtained at their office in Road Town, or at BVI customs offices and charter boat companies. When diving at sites without moorings, please exercise utmost caution when anchoring and avoid putting your anchor down in any reef area.

⑭ Arts, crafts and traditional industries

At one time, British Virgin Islanders were reliant on their own talents and skills to get by. These small islands separated by large tracts of sea were for centuries effectively isolated from the rest of the world. Boat building, charcoal making, salt harvesting, needlework and basket making were more than quaint traditions; they were day to day necessities. Today of course, planes and cargo ships bring in vast amounts of goods from around the globe, making some of these skills non-essential; but even so, many islanders continue to practise traditional island crafts, as well as some new ones. Tourism has opened up a whole new market for locally made goods, fuelling a renewed enthusiasm for the production of island-made crafts.

BOAT BUILDING
Tortola sloops and fishing skiffs

The Tortola sloop is a small traditional sailing boat unique to the British Virgin Islands. Its wide beam, sleek lines and sturdy mast make the sailing vessel not only elegant but highly functional. The sloop carried locally grown produce for sale in nearby St Thomas and brought back much-needed goods. They were also used for fishing – its wide, open hold is ideal for storing fish pots and nets. Several fine examples of the Tortola sloop are today owned by the H. Lavity Stoutt Community College and regularly participate in Foxy's Wooden Boat Regatta, an annual race held on Jost Van Dyke.

By the middle of the twentieth century, power vessels replaced sailing boats, and cars made transportation within the islands easier. Although the sloop was no longer built commercially in the latter half of the twentieth century, wooden fishing skiffs, low-freeboard wooden boats outfitted with outboards, are still constructed here on occasion. These brightly painted wooden fishing boats, often no more than 20 or so feet (6 metres) long, can be seen setting off from the shores of island fishing centres like Carrot Bay and East End.

Canoes

The sea has always been the life line of the BVI. From the Amerindians to the newly freed slaves, British Virgin Islanders have relied on the sea for their food and their transportation. The Amerindians fashioned their

▲ A net is stored at the back of a fishing boat

dugout canoes from hardwood trees, a laborious process that consisted of hollowing out large tree trunks by alternately charring and chopping them with stone axes known as celts. An example of a traditional Amerindian canoe, built in Dominica by BVI sculptor and artisan Aragorn Dick Read with the assistance of Dominican Carib Indians, is on display outside Aragorn's Studio on Beef Island. The artistically painted canoe, called the *Gli Gli*, is also available for day sails.

FISH POTS

The frames of these large, box-shaped cages were originally fashioned from the narrow branches of local hardwood trees and the sides from the woven leaves of the broom tyre palm. The traps are lowered into the water by a line attached to a marker buoy, most often a large plastic bleach bottle. Fish are lured into the trap's narrow, funnel-shaped opening by bait such as conch or whelk. It's a one-way trip, since once in, the fish cannot escape. Local fishermen still make their own fish pots, although the sides are now constructed of chicken wire, not palm fronds. Some original tyre palm fish pots are on display at the North Shore Shell Museum in Carrot Bay on Tortola.

CHARCOAL MAKING

Although less common than a decade ago, the pungent scent of a burning charcoal pit occasionally wafts through the air. Ever since the plantation era, farmers have used the brush and scrub cleared from local fields to make charcoal, an essential component of traditional cooking. Stacked and buried in large underground pits, the wood is set on fire and allowed to smoulder. Occasionally, the charcoal is used to fire the old stone ovens found in backyards around the island; but more often it is burned in the circular cast iron coal pots used for island picnics and fish fries. Because of its natural fragrance, residents also buy it for their home barbecues.

HAT WEAVING

For centuries, straw hats have adorned the heads of British Virgin Islands ladies for both church-going and as protection from the hot sun. Many still wear home-made straw hats, but they are more commonly produced these days for the tourist market. Like fish pots, straw hats are woven from the leaves of the broom tyre palm, which are dried in the sun for approximately a week. The dried palms are

▲ An array of locally made hats

woven into long, braid-like strands before being sewn together, a laborious process. The results, though, are light, fashionable and well worth the effort. Some of the finest examples of local hat making are by Estelle Dawson, whose creations can be found, among other places, at the Crafts Alive market in Road Town.

BASKET MAKING

The traditional BVI basket is made from the 'hoop vine', not straw. This robust vine makes a sturdy yet elegant basket that dries to a tawny colour. Examples of these baskets can be seen at Sunny Caribee on Main Street. Other locally made baskets and hats can be found at the BVI Handicraft Association shop at the Crafts Alive market as well as at the BVI Social Development Department shop next door.

POTTERY

Pottery was first fashioned in the BVI by its early Indian inhabitants. Local clay was made into both ceremonial and functional bowls and pots, many of which were decorated with adornos, intricately moulded figures on the rims and handles. Most plantation pottery was imported from England, and shards of plantation china and earthenware can sometimes be found near former plantation sites. In recent years, there has been a resurgence of pottery making as well as an improvement in the quality of the products. Pottery studios can be found throughout the islands, including Pat's Pottery on Anegada (her work is also sold in shops on Tortola), Bamboushay on Nanny Cay, where you can watch the potter at work in her studio, and Aragorn's Studio on Beef Island.

JEWELLERY MAKING

Hand-made jewellery, often crafted from local materials, is a popular industry. The materials used include the unique virgin jasper (a dark green stone found in the British Virgin Islands), coral, sea glass and seeds. Several studios around the islands produce and sell their own hand-crafted jewellery. Gold and silver items are also fashioned here.

OTHER HANDICRAFTS

The Crafts Alive market in Road Town, as well as gift shops around the BVI, feature hand-made dolls, dressed in traditional West Indian garb, and intricate local crochet work. Although some of these crafts are now imported from other Caribbean islands, many are still made here. Painted and embossed leather items, hand silk-screened fabrics, sarongs and tee-shirts, and locally produced fragrances and body products are also made in studios and craft shops around the islands.

NATIVE HOT SAUCES, SPICES AND RUMS

They may not be crafts, but these locally made items are a great way to take home the flavour of the islands. Sunny Caribbee on Main Street sells brightly packaged Caribbean spices, teas and condiments. Ashlely Nibbs, whose shop is located at the Crafts Alive market, sells a variety of home-made and potent hot sauces, as well as traditional guavaberry liqueur and gooseberry syrup. His family-run enterprise operates under the label, A. Nibbs Sons & Daughters. Pusser's Rum is the best known of our locally bottled rums and is sold in Pusser's Company stores throughout the islands. They also carry a line of hot sauces and other condiments. Island supermarkets sell other BVI produced hot sauces, jams and jellies as well as the locally bottled and flavourful Caribbean Spiced Rum. And if you're travelling to Jost Van Dyke, you should try Foxy's own label of rum and home-brewed beer.

▲ Ashley Nibbs displays his locally made products

⓯ When in the BVI

Practical information

The official language of these British islands is, not surprisingly, English. It may take a visitor a day or two to get the feel of the island cadence, especially when people are speaking fast. Rather than say 'hello', islanders generally say 'good morning', 'good afternoon' and 'good night', and if you want to get someone's attention, try prefacing your request with one of these phrases.

Dressing up is important in the BVI and for church the men often wear suits, no matter how warm the weather, and women dress elegantly in chiffons, silks and often hats in lovely pastels or tropical colours. Dress for funerals (which are generally large in these family-oriented islands) is black, white, or a combination of the two.

The dress code for visitors is simple. Shorts, tee shirts and other cool casual clothing are the norm for day. A very few restaurants require long trousers for men in the evening, and women might want to pack a skirt or dress for a special dinner out. Wearing scanty clothing and bathing suits anywhere other than the beach is frowned upon in these modest islands.

'BELONGERS' AND 'NON-BELONGERS'

Visitors often wonder what these terms mean, and if you are going to spend any time here, it is helpful to understand the difference. If you are from elsewhere, you are definitely a 'non-belonger'. This would be both visitors and residents who have not been naturalized. Belongers are those who are native-born British Virgin Islanders, but they are also outsiders who have had the status conferred on them through naturalization. Property holders can apply for a special non-working residency status that needs to be renewed annually. 'Down Islanders' are residents of the British Virgin Islands who come from Caribbean islands to the south of the BVI.

A WORD ABOUT DRIVING

A temporary driver's licence is necessary to drive in the BVI; it can be procured at most rental car businesses or the Licensing Department in Road Town for the cost of $10. One of the most important things to remember when in the BVI is that we drive on the left, a tradition brought across the Atlantic from Britain. Oddly though, our cars are mainly imported from the US, so that the steering wheel is also on the left. When on the road, drivers should watch out for two unexpected hazards: speed bumps which slow traffic down in residential areas and can crop up when you least expect them, and animals. A herd of cows being driven down the road is not unusual, and goats and sheep seem to have no road sense at all, darting across the road impulsively.

When in the BVI remember that life here is at a 'don't worry, it'll get done' pace, and driving is no exception. When two cars stop in the middle of the road so the drivers can have a conversation, you will rarely hear a car horn honk to hasten them on their way. Also it is customary here to stop for pedestrians on a crossing.

WHAT TO BUY AND WHERE TO BUY IT

Visitors don't generally come to the British Virgin Islands for the shopping; with so many beautiful beaches, why should they? The BVI is not a duty free port and doesn't have a lot of glitzy stores, but nonetheless there are a number of very nice boutiques and speciality shops carrying bright and breezy tropical clothing, and even French

▲ A shop in Jost Van Dyke

fashions. You will find Indonesian gift and home items, Mexican pottery and items from Africa and the Orient. Some firms produce and package their own unique BVI lines of goods including the Pusser's Company Store, which has its own brand of rum as well as apparel; Sunny Caribbee, which packages Caribbean spices, coffees, teas and condiments on the premises; and HIHO, which markets its own brand of surfwear. Caribbean Essence located at the Crafts Alive market in Road Town locally produces its own bath and body products and fragrances. Throughout the islands you will find dozens of other unique shops carrying great items to help you remember your trip.

The main shopping areas in Road Town are on Main Street, which has several boutiques and shops located in West Indian style houses; and Wickhams Cay, a large reclaimed area adjacent to the harbour. On Tortola, there are also shopping areas near Road Reef Marina, Nanny Cay Marina, Soper's Hole Marina, Cane Garden Bay, Hodges Creek Marina and Trellis Bay. Virgin Gorda has shopping areas at the Yacht Harbour, in the Valley, at the Top of The Baths and Leverick Bay. You will also find interesting boutiques at resorts, restaurants and hotels throughout the islands.

HOW'S THE WEATHER?

Almost always good. British Virgin Islands weather reports generally make dull listening: 'Today will be mostly sunny, the winds are from the southeast at 8 to 10 knots and the chance of precipitation is 20 per cent.' Those famous tradewinds that blow between 25 and 30 degrees north of the equator and were vital to early shipping are also responsible for the cooling breezes that blow from the southeast virtually year-round, making the BVI's climate pleasant, even in summer. The temperature range in the islands varies little more than 10 degrees between winter and summer. Winter temperatures average 70 degrees in the evening and 80 degrees in the day; while summer temps run in the 80s at night and low to mid-90s in the day.

These are semi-tropical islands and our rainfall is inconsistent, which is great for visitors. Most showers are intermittent, and may last just 10 or 15 minutes. They can also be highly localized. Amazingly, it may pour in Road Town, but neighbouring Sea Cows Bay won't get a drop. November and May are said to be the rainiest months, but even on a cloudy day the sun will usually appear for at least part of the day. It also rains a bit more along the upper levels of Tortola, especially beneath Sage Mountain, our highest point, and less on the Tortola's East End and outer islands, which tend to be drier.

ARRIVING HERE AND STAYING HERE: ENTRY REQUIREMENTS

It's important to arrive in the BVI with the right documentation, although for most visitors, the procedure is straightforward. In the majority of cases, visitors will be granted entry for a maximum of four weeks. A valid passport is required for all visitors to the BVI, including British, US and Canadian citizens. To stay longer than a month, you will need to get special permission from the BVI Department of Immigration. Visitors from some countries may need a visa for entry (although not if you are from the US, Canada, UK and most countries in Europe). To check on entry requirements, or determine if you need a visa, please contact a BVI Tourist Board office, or the BVI Department of Immigration in Road Town, Tortola (tel: 284-494-3471 or 284-468-3701).

If you decide to work here, you will have to apply for a work permit. It's also possible to buy land in the BVI, but a Non-Belonger's Landholding Licence is required before ownership is conferred; this, as with most bureaucratic procedures, can take a while.

PERMITS, FEES AND TAXES

If you are sailing or cruising here, you will need a cruising permit, which can cost from $0.75 to $4.00 per day, depending on the type of boat and if it's high or low season. Yachtsmen should contact the BVI Customs Department for current cruising permit requirements.

To protect our reefs and underwater environment, boats are required to use the National Parks Trust's mooring buoys, which have been installed at popular anchorages and diving areas. Permits can be purchased at the National Parks Trust office on Main Street in Road Town. Buoys have been installed at key areas on the following islands: Tortola, Virgin Gorda, Peter, Norman, Salt, Cooper, Scrub, Dead Chest, Ginger, Fallen Jerusalem, the Dogs, Great Camanoe, Norman, Great Tobago, Green Cay, Pelican, the Indians and at the wreck of the *Chikuzen*. For more information call the NPT office on 284-494-3904.

Protecting our fisheries and marine life is also of paramount importance and the removal of any marine organism from our waters is illegal for non-British Virgin Islanders without a fishing permit. Call the Department of Conservation and Fisheries on 284-494-3429 for further information on obtaining a permit. There is no anchoring or fishing permitted at the Wreck of the *Rhone* Marine Park.

Certain national parks, including The Baths, the Botanic Gardens and Sage Mountain charge small entry fees ranging from $1 to $3 for individuals. There are also multiple use and BVI resident (ID required) rates. For a complete schedule of fees, contact the National Parks Trust in Road Town (tel: 284-494-3904).

A departure tax of $15 is charged for each passenger leaving by air. There is also a $5 per person security tax. The departure tax for passengers leaving by sea is $5; $7 for cruise ship passengers.

There is no sales tax in the BVI, but a customs duty ranging from 5 per cent to 20 per cent is charged for all newly purchased goods arriving (and staying) on the island. Imports entering on a temporary basis are not subject to duty.

CURRENCY, CREDIT CARDS AND BANKS

The BVI uses the US dollar as currency. Major credit cards, including Visa, Mastercard and American Express, are accepted at most establishments, although a few of the smaller bars and restaurants may accept cash only or traveller's cheques. If using a traveller's cheque, don't be surprised if you are charged an extra 10 cents; there is a 10 cent stamp duty on all bank cheques and traveller's cheques. Traveller's cheques can be cashed at banks. The main retail banks include: First Bank Virgin Islands, Banco Popular de Puerto Rico, First Caribbean Bank and Scotiabank (BVI).

WEDDING BELLS

Getting married in the BVI is growing in popularity. What could be more romantic than a wedding on a beautiful white sand beach

▲ A beachside wedding

or in an open air restaurant adjacent to the crystal blue waters of the Caribbean? Couples have even been married here on yachts, underwater and, of course, in one of our many beautiful churches. To tie the knot in the BVI you must apply for a marriage licence, which will take three days to process. If you want to be married by the Registrar, book prior to your arrival by calling the office ahead of time; application for the ceremony must be made after the licence has been granted. The Registrar will perform the ceremony in his office in Road Town, although for an additional fee, plus transportation, the Registrar will travel to the site of your choice (within reason). Several wedding planners are located in the BVI and some of the larger hotels and resorts will also assist with wedding arrangements. For complete requirements, fees and documentation for getting married in the BVI, contact the Registrar's Office on 284-468-3701.

GOING TO CHURCH

Most of the major denominations as well as some smaller ones are represented in the BVI. Among the many churches found here are

▲ A church at Great Harbour, Jost Van Dyke

Anglican (Episcopalian), Methodist, Roman Catholic, Baptist, Seventh Day Adventist, Church of God, Jehovah's Witness and Pentecostal Church of Christ.

MEDICAL MATTERS

You do not need an international vaccination certificate to enter the BVI. The health services include Peebles Hospital in Road Town which has surgical, emergency, X-Ray and laboratory facilities. There are also several private medical clinics and laboratories, including B & F Medical Complex, Eureka Medical Clinic, Medical Diagnostic Laboratory and the Bougainvillea Clinic, which specializes in plastic and general surgery. The Community Agency on Drugs and Addiction (CADA) holds meetings for Alcoholics Anonymous, Narcotics Anonymous and Overeaters Anonymous. For information call 284-494-3125.

FREQUENTLY ASKED QUESTIONS
Can I use my hair dryer?
The BVI's voltage is 110 (American system), so if you are coming from the UK or Europe you will need a converter. There is some 220 volt for heavy equipment use.

And can I drink the water?
The water, which is drinkable, is primarily desalinated and then treated. Some though, especially in private homes, is rain water that has been collected from the roof and stored in cisterns. Purified water, either locally bottled, or imported, is sold at most markets.

What about bringing a pet?
If you are only here for a short time, it's best to leave pets at home. If you do want to bring a pet in, you will need an import permit issued by the Department of Agriculture. For regulations and further information on importing an animal, contact (well in advance) the Department of Agriculture, 284-495-2532.

OTHER USEFUL CONTACTS AND TELEPHONE NUMBERS
Emergency and medical
For police, fire or ambulance service, dial 999 or 911.

Virgin Islands Search and Rescue (VISAR) performs rescue at sea. In an emergency call VHF Channel 16, or dial 767 from a local telephone. From outside the BVI call 284-499-0911.

Government of the British Virgin Islands
Most departments of the BVI Government can be reached through its main switchboard, tel: 284-468-3701. To write to a specific

department you should specify the department name and send to: Government of the British Virgin Islands, Road Town, Tortola, British Virgin Islands.

Dept of Civil Aviation / BVI Airport Authority

For information on airport operation tel: (284) 494-6494.

BVI Tourist Board Offices in the British Virgin Islands

In Road Town, the BVI Tourist Board is located on Wickhams Cay; they also have visitor centres at the ferry dock in the centre of town and at the Terrence B. Lettsome International Airport on Beef Island. Contact information for some of the main Tourist Board offices is listed below.

BVI Tourist Board Road Town: tel: 284-494-3134; fax 284-494-3866; email: info@bvitourism.com; mailing address: PO Box 134, Road Town, Tortola, British Virgin Islands.

Virgin Gorda: Virgin Gorda Yacht Harbour; tel: 284-495-5181.

UK: 15 Upper Grosvenor St, London W1K 7PJ; tel: 207-355-9585; fax: 207-355-9587; email: infouk@bvi.org.uk

New York: 1270 Broadway, Suite 705, New York, NY 10001; tel: 212-696-0400; fax: 212-563-2263; email: info@bvitourism.com; toll free US number: 800-835-8530.

Once you arrive on the island, the *BVI Welcome Tourist Guide* provides informative articles on island life, as well as information on dining, shopping, hotels, accommodation, yacht charters and dive operators. The *Welcome* also has a comprehensive website: www.bviwelcome.com. The *BVI Restaurant Guide* offers menus and information about local foods and restaurants, and the *Limin Times* is a local entertainment weekly. Published by Island Publishing Services, Road Town, these guides are available free of charge at points of entry, hotels, charter boat firms and elsewhere around the islands. They can be purchased in advance of your stay by contacting Island Publishing Services, PO Box 133, Road Town, Tortola, BVI for a cost of $6 US. To order by phone by credit card, call 284-494-2413 or order online at www.bviwelcome.com.

The *BVI Tourism Directory* produced by the BVI Tourist Board has a comprehensive list of accommodation, services and yacht charter companies and is available through the BVI Tourist Board offices worldwide. For additional BVI Tourist Board offices worldwide go to its website: www.bvitourism.com.

ISLAND EVENTS

The BVI has entertainment at clubs and restaurants year-round. In addition, there are a number of special festivals and events. A few of the biggest follow.

Generally held the first weekend of April, the **BVI Spring Regatta** is the BVI's premier sailing event, attracting racing yachtsmen from around the world. It is co-sponsored by the BVI Yacht Club (tel: 284-494-3286) and the BVI Chamber of Commerce and Hotel Association (tel: 284-494-3514).

Although not as big as Tortola's Emancipation Festival in August, the **Virgin Gorda Easter Festival** is a lot of fun. There is local food, music, dance and a parade over the three-day Easter weekend. Call the BVI Tourist Board, 284-494-3134, for details.

An island tradition, **Foxy's Wooden Boat Race**, sponsored by Foxy's on Jost Van Dyke, attracts wooden sailing yachts from throughout the Virgin Islands. It is held on the last weekend of May. For more information call Foxy's, 284-495-9258.

Island music and top international reggae, jazz and popular bands gather on the beach at Cane Garden Bay for the **BVI Music Festival**, a musical extravaganza held on the last weekend of May. Call the BVI Tourist Board for more information, 284-494-3134.

The **BVI Emancipation Festival** consists of two weeks of local entertainment, food and celebrations culminating in a Grand Parade during the last week of July and the first week of August. Call the BVI Tourist Board for dates and information: 284-494-3134.

The **HIHO** is an island to island windsurfing race covering most of the British Virgins. It is held the first week of July. Call HIHO at 284-494-0337 for dates and information.

The **Christmas Steel Band Concert and Fungi Fiesta** is held mid-December in Road Town. Call the BVI Tourist Board, 284-494-3134 for dates and venues.

For a complete calendar of events contact the BVI Tourist Board (tel: 284-494-3134). All the above information is intended as a guide only and is subject to change.

The BVI Spring Regatta

Appendix

The geological origins of the British Virgin Islands by Jim Rogers

This island chain, the Lesser Antilles, forms the leading edge of a giant oceanic mass called the Caribbean plate, moving at a minute but steady speed eastward, overriding the adjacent Atlantic Oceanic plate. The inexorable turmoil caused at this massive plate junction (which geologists call a subduction zone) has generated violent volcanic eruptions (some, like Montserrat, active today) which have produced and enlarged most of the islands.

Unlike the rest of the archipelago, the Virgin Islands have not been influenced by recent (in geological terms) volcanic activity. The Virgin Islands sit on the Virgin Island platform, a broad east–west shelf of shallow seas (always less than 600 feet deep) at the northeast corner of the Caribbean Sea. The platform is 'rooted' on a foundation of sea-floor basalt flows (basalt is a dark, dense, fine-grained rock) deposited more than 80 million years ago at great water depths beneath the sea. Later many thousands of feet of volcanic sediments including (rocks now called) andesite breccias, pyroclastic sandstones and tuffs accumulated on this basalt flow. (Geologists are not certain of the source of these volcanic sediments; the trace of the equivalent ancient volcanic activity has been obscured by time.) Most of the volcanic sediments were deposited in near-horizontal layers on the sea floor, but through later powerful uplifts were tilted to a near vertical position.

About 40 million years ago an initial uplift of great thicknesses of ancient sea-floor sediments was generated by the insertion of a large mass of hot, liquid magma called a batholith, which arched the layers of sediment into a great elongated dome beneath the eastern part of the Virgin Island platform. This hot liquid deposit (now called the Virgin Gorda Batholith) slowly cooled beneath the arch of sediments, thus the term 'intrusive', as opposed to volcanic eruptions which generate 'extrusive' igneous rocks. In the BVI intrusive rocks are described by geologists as varieties of granite, more specifically granodiorite, tonalite and diorite. We can see these (mostly) coarse-crystalline granite rocks clearly today because intense weathering and erosion through many subsequent ages has removed most of the dome or arch of sediments that once covered the intrusion. At no place are the granites of the Virgin Gorda Batholith more dramatically displayed today than at the Virgin Gorda Baths. This great batholith was not restricted to Virgin Gorda; today we find large granite outcrops at Beef Island, Camanoe, Scrub Island, Peter and Cooper Islands, and even far to the west along the north shore of St John and at the east end of St Thomas, both in the US Virgin Islands. In fact most geologists believe that eroded granite still underlies most of the Sir Francis Drake Channel, which runs the length of the BVI.

Subsequent to the initial tilting of the older volcanic sediments caused by the intrusion of the batholith, additional tectonic forces due to younger plate movements pushed the original dome or arch (with its long axis oriented east–west) into an even steeper aspect. For that reason, most of the volcanic rocks exposed on Tortola are now in a near-vertical position. Furthermore, most BVI outcrops of volcanic rocks are aligned and more resistant in an east–west direction, and it is this orientation that has given many of the smaller Virgin islands (i.e. the Thatch Islands and the Congo Keys) their east–west elongation.

Jim Rogers is a geologist who is a part-time resident of Virgin Gorda; he has been studying the geology of the BVI for over ten years. Much of the above information is based on a 1961 Princeton PhD thesis by Charles E. Helsley.